AN AUTHOR'S GUIDE
TO PUBLISHING

Michael Legat was born in London and educated
at the Whitgift School, Croydon. He joined the
Publicity and Production Departments of The
Bodley Head in 1941, and apart from three years
service in the Navy, stayed there for nine years. In
1952 he was appointed Editorial Director of Corgi
Books, following which he held the same position
with Cassell & Company. For the past nine years
he has been a full-time author, publisher's consul-
tant and lecturer. He is married with two children,
and lives in Horsted Keynes.

An Author's Guide to Publishing

by

Michael Legat

ROBERT HALE · LONDON

© *Michael Legat 1982*
First published in Great Britain 1982
Reprinted 1982
Reprinted 1984
First paperback edition (with revisions) 1987

ISBN 0 7090 0510 5 (cased edition)
ISBN 0 7090 3067 3 (paperback edition)

Robert Hale Limited
Clerkenwell House
Clerkenwell Green
London EC1R 0HT

British Library Cataloguing in Publication Data
Legat, Michael
 An author's guide to publishing.
 1. Authorship   2. Publishers and publishing
 – Great Britain
 I. Title
 070.5′0941   PN145

Typeset by Rowland Phototypesetting Limited
Printed in Great Britain by St Edmundsbury Press Limited
Bury St Edmunds, Suffolk and
bound by Woolnough Bookbinding Limited

Contents

To the memory of C. J. and of Peter
and to all my friends in the writing business,
whether they are authors or agents or
publishers or booksellers or critics or
whatever,
and of course to Rosetta

Foreword

This book is invaluable reading for all authors – and not simply beginners and those without agents. While obviously the Society cannot endorse everything that Michael Legat says we can thoroughly recommend his book as a balanced, helpful and informative guide to the profession of authorship.

Philippa MacLiesh
Mark Le Fanu
The Society of Authors

Author's Note

I wish to make it clear that the ideas put forward in this book are not necessarily those of its publisher, nor of my other publishers, nor of my agent, nor of any publishing firm for which I have worked, nor of the Society of Authors nor of any other authors' organization. They are mine alone, so no blame will attach to the reader if he regards them with a certain suspicion. The views are, however, based on over forty years' experience of the book trade, and I hope therefore that the suspicion will not be justified too often.

I have used male pronouns throughout, and I apologize to the feminists for wanting to avoid the constant clumsiness of "he or she", "himself or herself", "his or her", and so on. Please read in the alternatives whenever appropriate. I do not in any way wish to suggest an inequality between the sexes in the world of books. Like many another dedicated reader, I do not choose my books according to the sex of the author, and I applaud the fact that no one any longer sneers, as they may have done in past generations, at women writers, or expect them to be any less capable as authors than men; as for publishers and agents, there are many women in their ranks who are at least as perceptive and expert and effective as their male colleagues, if not more so – though they may also be rather more formidable and even terrifying, partly because, as one wit put it, "the trouble with business women is that they aren't always gentlemen".

I should like to express my thanks to Philippa MacLiesh and Mark Le Fanu of the Society of Authors for their invaluable assistance and advice; to John McLaughlin and John Hale for their helpful comments and suggestions; to Ian Rowland Hill of the Writers' Guild of Great Britain for additional help; to Robin Denniston for allowing me to quote from his paper given to a meeting of the University, College and Research Section of the Library Association; and to the

Hutchinson Publishing Group Ltd, for permission to quote a short extract from *Allen Lane: King Penguin* by Jack Morpurgo.

M. L.

1

The World of Books

Territories and Rights

Even those whose knowledge of geography is minimal are aware that the world is divided into the continents of Europe, Asia, North and South America, Africa and Australia, to which may be added the Arctic and Antarctic and a large number of islands scattered through the oceans and seas. The author who writes in English may need to learn a different kind of geography. For him, the world is likely to be divided into three: the exclusive British market, the exclusive American (i.e. United States) market, and the rest of the world, which is termed the Open market.

Until a few years ago, these divisions were easily defined: the British market consisted of the United Kingdom and the British Empire, including all its colonies and protectorates and a number of countries, such as Egypt and Iraq, where the British influence had been traditionally strong; the American market consisted of the United States of America and its colonies and protectorates; Canada was normally exclusive to the British publisher if the book were of British or British Empire origin, and exclusive to the American publisher if it were of United States origin; the rest of the world was non-exclusive territory. Even after the British Empire became the Commonwealth and certain countries such as South Africa and Malta became independent republics, the British publisher's traditional market remained a recognized entity. In the 1970s, however, at the instigation of the United States, it was agreed that the split of territories between the British and the American publisher should be re-defined in the case of each book, and the fact that a given country had been traditionally part of the exclusive market of one of the publishers should no longer mean that it was necessarily so for every book. Some territories which had always been regarded as belonging to the Open market could become part of the

British or American publisher's exclusive area, and the growth of publishing industries in places like Australia, which previously relied almost entirely on Britain for its books, has further fragmented the old divisions. In the majority of cases, however, of a book which is published both in Britain and the United States, the world is still divided into three, with some territories exclusive to the British or the American publisher, and the remaining countries open to them both.

Within the British exclusive territory the British publisher sells his edition of the book without competition from his American rival; equally, only the American publisher's edition sells in the American exclusive territory; in the Open market, however, both the British and the American publishers can sell their editions of the same book in direct competition with each other.

An additional problem has arisen recently as a result of Britain's membership of the EEC. Since trade barriers are prohibited within the Common Market, it is possible for a European wholesaler to purchase copies of a given book from the American publisher and then export them to Britain, thus infringing the British publisher's exclusivity in his home market, but relying on the provisions of the Treaty of Rome to be stronger than the agreement regarding territories between the British and American publishers. The enterprise can be profitable to the wholesaler because of the fact that the British and American retail prices may differ considerably, and whereas in the past the British price was usually below that of the American edition, the reverse is often now the case. Fluctuations in exchange rates make this a volatile situation. Because of the dangers to them, some British publishers attempt from time to time to add the EEC to their exclusive market, thus preventing the American publisher from selling the book in question there, and obviating the threat of an invasion of the home territory. It should be pointed out that the issue is one of market violation and not necessarily of infringement of the author's copyright. However, since in many cases it is the author who grants his various publishers, initially, their territories, whether exclusive or non-exclusive, he may become involved in any dispute between them.

Foreign language publishers do not have the same problems of sharing out the world as English language publishers do. A German publisher, for instance, will usually have the whole world available to him for his German language edition of a book, and most foreign language publishers, but not all, have exclusive rights throughout the world.

Incidentally, it should be made clear that sales of a British or American, or indeed Australian or Indian, English language publication in a foreign language country has nothing to do with Foreign Language rights, or Translation rights, as they are sometimes called, which refer to translations into a foreign language. Although the book may be on sale in France or Germany or Japan, if it is in the British or American English language edition then it comes under the British or American publisher's export sales, not under Foreign rights.

If you write in English and sell your book directly to a publisher in Britain or the United States, he will probably buy world rights. He will then attempt to sell either the American or the British rights in the book to a publisher on the other side of the Atlantic, and the details of the territories which will be exclusive and non-exclusive to each will be decided at the time of the sale. However, if an agent is involved, he will normally retain on the author's behalf the American rights (or in the case of an American author and agent, the British rights), which he, the agent, will then attempt to sell. It is difficult to say which of the two methods is preferable, since it depends on the abilities of the agents and publishers concerned, though the agent will probably take a slightly smaller share of any moneys earned from the sale of US (or British) rights. If the transatlantic rights are not sold, then in rare cases the British edition may be put on sale in the US (or vice versa), but the resulting sales are usually minimal.

Whatever the territories granted to him, the British or American publisher normally expects to control a large number of rights in the book. The copyright in the book usually remains the property of the author, and should do so (see p. 29), but the right to sell the book in various forms is vested in the publisher. If he buys direct from an author, he will usually ask for control of all rights, which is to say that he not only has the right to produce various editions of the book, or to license others to do so, but also that he can sell serial rights, anthology rights, film, radio and television and a number of other subsidiary rights, in each case passing to the author an agreed share of the proceeds from such sales. If he buys the book from an agent, it is likely that he will be restricted to volume rights, which is to say the right to produce, or license others to produce, hardcover or paperback editions of the book, to sell bookclub rights, and usually second serial (i.e. serial rights sold after the first publication in book form) and anthology rights, the sale of all such rights often being subject to the agent's approval, all other rights being retained in the control of the agent and sold by him on the author's behalf. However, nowadays the hardcover publisher cannot even be certain of volume rights, for sometimes paperback rights are sold separately by the agent. Of course it is open to the author who deals directly with the publisher to retain various rights if he wishes to do so and if the publisher is still willing to publish the book on those terms, but there is little point in so doing unless the author is himself equipped to sell the rights in question. Few publishers make no effort at all to sell the rights they are granted, for the very good reason that their share of any moneys resulting from such sales increases their profit or at worst diminishes their losses on the book in question.

It is very important, whatever arrangements have been made, to remember what rights you have granted to your publisher. If, for instance, you have given him the right to negotiate foreign language rights, and you then happen to meet a charming French publisher who expresses great interest in your book, you must not sell him your book, or even give him an option on it, and indeed it would be wise, I suggest, not even to give him a copy to read unless you make it perfectly clear that doing so does not commit your publisher in any way. Apart from the fact that you have handed control of foreign rights to your publisher and are therefore going against your contractual commitments, you may also cause quite a lot of embarrassment, especially, for instance, if your publisher is in the midst of delicate negotiations over the book with another French publisher. Instead, you should thank your French friend for his interest, tell him that you will let your publisher know of it, and do so. The same applies, of course, if it is your agent who has control of the rights. If the French publisher's interest is genuine (and do bear in mind that it could have been merely polite), and the book is not in the hands of another French publisher, your publisher or agent will probably be happy to submit it to your friend straight away, or to send it as soon as it is free of other commitments.

Licence Periods

In most publishing contracts, the author gives the publisher the various rights defined in the agreement "for the period of copyright". This last phrase may be further defined by some such wording as "and all renewals and extensions thereof in each country". The effect, in most cases, is to give the publisher the rights in the book from the time of publication until fifty years after the author's death. If he goes on selling the book, he will of course go on paying the specified royalties to the author or, eventually, his heirs. If he does not keep the book in print, and/or under certain other circumstances which are usually clearly defined in the contract, the rights will revert to the author, though the publisher may be able to retain the rights if the book is still in print in an edition which he has sub-licensed. There is currently a move, led by the Society of Authors and the Writers' Guild and some agents, to restrict the licence to a much shorter period, such as ten years, with an option for its renewal. (See p. 110.) One of the arguments used in pressing this change is that publishers themselves, when granting sub-licences to paperback houses, bookclubs and the like, generally do so for a strictly limited period only.

Hardcover Books

Books are sold in a variety of formats, and though there is some overlap in the markets for hardcover books, paperbacks, bookclub editions, condensed books and so on, it would appear that they are not totally competitive. Thus bookclubs, for instance, claim that their members are not on the whole regular buyers of hardcover books, and that they are therefore tapping a new, or at least different, market; equally there must be many thousands of homes where you will find large numbers of paperbacks but never a recent hardcover book in sight, apart perhaps from a mail order *Book of the Countryside* or something similar.

There are several hundred hardcover book publishers in Britain, publishing an infinite variety of books. Some are specialist publishers, producing perhaps only medical or legal or school books, while others have a general list embracing fiction and non-fiction of all kinds, but also including sometimes books in a specialist field. Some are huge companies, bringing out hundreds of new books every year, while others are one-man concerns, publishing only one or two books a season. Some hardcover publishers also publish paperback editions of certain of the books on their list, but these are usually no more than cheap editions, and cannot be considered as mass-market paperbacks.

Print quantities of hardcover books vary enormously, and so do the retail prices of the books, ranging from a few score copies of an extremely expensive limited edition, to fifty thousand or more copies of a major bestseller, which may be comparatively cheap. Nowadays very few books achieve a print quantity of more than fifty thousand in their hardcover editions. The majority of the books on a general publisher's list are likely to have initial print runs of between two and a half thousand and ten thousand copies, and the prices will be in a limited and familiar range.

Hardcover publishers sell their books primarily to bookshops and to libraries. The sad decline of bookshops (we are all accustomed to the encroachment of records, toys and gift items on spaces previously devoted to books), the shrinkage of the library market (money for books is always one of the first targets for local councillors seeking ways of cutting their budget), the more competitive situation in Britain's export outlets (sales of hardcover books to Australia and South Africa, for instance, have dropped dramatically during the last decade), coupled with the difficulty of preserving a backlist (the cost of capital investment means that it is often impossible to reprint worthwhile but slow-moving books) – all these factors have made the hardcover publisher's life extremely difficult, and there are many pundits who forecast the imminent disappearance of new hardcover books, which they say will soon be replaced by sound and video cassettes. The death of the hardcover book has been predicted for many, many years now, but it has managed to survive, and though the arguments against its continuance are perhaps stronger now than they have been in the past, I believe that it is far from done for yet.

Its survival could be guaranteed for a longer period, of course, if sales of the average book could be substantially increased. Despite the belief of some authors to the contrary, publishers do make efforts to sell their books – a book sitting on the warehouse shelf is of no use to anyone, and indeed it actually costs the publisher money to keep it there – and they try, by means of special book events and the willing support they give, for example, to television programmes about books, to promote sales. However, it has to be admitted that the bulk of the public remains untouched, and will probably be very difficult to convert. In the Church of England there is something called Christian Stewardship, under which the supporter of the church promises to give a certain sum of money every week for the work of the church, and similar schemes operate in other denominations. I believe that an arrangement of the same kind should come into being to encourage those who are already committed to buying hard-cover books to buy more. Under Book Stewardship, a weekly sum would be put aside to be spent on hardcover books, additional to the books that the saver would have bought anyway. Since authors have a vested interest in keeping books alive, they should be the first to support such a scheme; it will benefit them by keeping the hardcover business in a thriving state, and it will also put a few extra pennies into the pockets of other authors, no doubt as impecunious as themselves. Why spend the money on hardcover books rather than paper-backs? Because although the paperback publishers also live on a knife-edge of profitability, for reasons which I shall discuss later, they already have a much larger slice of the reading market, and it would need hundreds of thousands of new buyers to enlarge their sales significantly, whereas far fewer could have a marked effect on hardcover sales; more importantly, because, although paperback publishers do origi-nate books (i.e. publish in paperback books which have not previously been published in hardback), it is still primarily the hardcover publisher who invests in new talent and in long-term projects, and who frequently takes a great risk in doing so.

The bulk of sales on a general list, and this applies particu-larly to fiction, will be sold on publication and in the first six months thereafter. Bestsellers may have a longer life, and some books are fortunate enough to become backlist titles or standard works, and will go on selling steadily for a period of years. They are the exceptions, as are those very few books which suddenly come to vigorous life long after the initial impetus has disappeared (frequently because of a television series based on the book, such as *The Forsyte Saga* or *I, Claudius* and *Claudius the God*, or because, as in the case of *Jonathan Livingston Seagull*, it has become a "cult" book, or for some other equally unpredictable reason). Interest in an author's earlier books can sometimes be revived if he writes a particularly successful new book, which happened in the case of that fine novelist Paul Scott, after he won the Booker Prize with his novel *Staying On*. In most cases, however, the author of a book will find that a very high proportion of the total sales he achieves will be shown on the first royalty statement that he receives after the book's publication, and indeed if the book came out at the beginning of the royalty period, the proportion may be as high as 80 or 90 per cent.

Many of those sales will have been to libraries. Demand has diminished substantially in recent years, not only because of cuts in local council spending but also because the libraries have improved their services to borrowers so that a single copy of a book can be more readily available in any branch of a group of libraries, whereas in the past that group would have purchased several copies and spread them around the branches. Nevertheless, British libraries have always been, and look like remaining, the best in the world. No other country has so extensive and well-stocked a system of public libraries, making books available at no cost (except indirectly to the ratepayer) to everyone. We may justly be proud of them as one of our greater national glories, but they are also a considerable millstone around the necks of publishers and authors, for they have turned us into a nation of book borrowers rather than book buyers. We have one of the smallest annual *per capita* book purchase figures among the affluent nations. How many authors have despaired at hearing their friends promise to get their books out of the library?

Hardcover publishers sell their books to libraries either in bound form or in sheets which are then bound by library suppliers, though the latter method is far more rare nowadays than it used to be. Whether the library buys a bound book or a set of sheets, the author receives a royalty only on that single sale, no matter how many times the book is borrowed and read, and naturally he feels hard done by. The publishers may also complain that their return from the single sale is unfair, considering what use will be made of the book, but few would argue that this case is as strong as the author's.

For several years now there has been a campaign to introduce the Public Lending Right, under which authors would receive additional payments for the borrowing of their books from public libraries. Successive politicians have helped or hampered the progress of the Bill, but by the time this book is published PLR should at last be operative. It is not likely to make many authors rich, and indeed there is some fear that most of the funds available will be swallowed up by the most popular authors, benefiting primarily those who are already successful. However, a limited number of other writers should receive reasonably healthy sums, and even those who do not come into that category should rejoice that authors will at last be getting some return from the library-borrowings of their books. We should be very grateful to the Society of Authors, whose officers and members have been battling for PLR since 1951, to the Writers' Action Group, which, led by Brigid Brophy and Maureen Duffy, spearheaded the attack in most recent years, and to the Writers' Guild, and to all their supporters whose efforts have finally resulted in this recognition of authors' rights. Incidentally, it is worth noting that it was John Brophy, Brigid's father, who first pleaded for payment for authors on library-borrowings, with his "A Penny a Book" campaign, in which he was greatly supported by A. P. Herbert.

Some publishers, incidentally, are asking their authors to share with them any income from PLR. The Society of Authors, the Writers' Guild and, I would imagine, all agents would advise authors against agreeing to any split of these rights.

Paperbacks

There are far fewer paperback publishers than hardcover houses, with perhaps no more than a score of major imprints in this country. Some of them are owned by hardcover houses, or have close links with them, but they are usually separately managed and do not only publish books which have first appeared on the lists of their parent companies. On the whole, paperback publishers concentrate on very popular books, and fiction predominates, though most of them also produce children's books and have other specialist sections on their lists.

Paperbacks are of course very much cheaper than hardcover books – not, as many people believe, because the thin board cover and the binding process used (known as "perfect binding", the back edges of the signatures, or folded sheets, being guillotined off and the separate pages of the book then glued together, whereas the hardcover book is still likely to have its signatures sewn together before the binding case is drawn on) are much cheaper than the boards and cloth and more complex binding of hardcover books, but because the paperback business is predicated upon large quantities. The minimum print quantity for a paperback book is usually in the region of fifteen to twenty thousand, and bestsellers may well be produced in quantities up to a million. Certainly the paper is of poorer quality and the binding is somewhat cheaper and the author's royalty rates are usually lower than for hardcover books, but it is the mass production of large quantities which keeps the retail price down. The publisher's profit may well be calculated in several decimal places of one penny, but since he sells so many copies his sales income is sufficient to cover his overheads and give him a net profit and to provide for the large sums he often spends on the promotion of his best-sellers.

Paperbacks are of course very widely sold in regular book-shops, but they are also available in newsagents' and sweet-shops, and increasingly in supermarkets, tobacconists, hair-dressers, and other non-traditional outlets. Libraries too are beginning to take paperbacks in substantial numbers. Although paperback publishers do sell directly to some retail-ers, the bulk of their sales is made to wholesalers, who supply and service the thousands of small retail customers for the books, or to the central buying offices of the big chains.

The rights in the majority of paperback books are still bought from hardcover publishers, and though there are examples of both editions being published simultaneously, it is more usual for there to be a gap between the appearance of the hardcover book and that of the paperback of at least six months and more often a year or longer. This delay is imposed by hardcover publishers because, although it is true that paperback buyers are not in the main buyers of hardcovers, hardcover buyers can easily be seduced into the purchase of paperbacks, and hardcover publishers believe that publica-tion of a paperback edition simultaneously with or very shortly after their own publication date does damage their sales. With major books, especially those of American origin, it is commonplace for the paperback edition to be published overseas in the Open market very much earlier than for the domestic market, and this is done in order to meet the competition of the American paperback edition of the same book, and indeed the British and American houses are often engaged in warfare over these lucrative export markets, each trying to produce his edition first so as to capture the bulk of the sales. It is as true of paperbacks as of hardcovers that, except with the most durable titles, the larger part of the sales will be achieved during the first six months after publication.

Although paperback publishers obtain most of their books from hardcover publishers, they publish an increasing number of "originals" (books published for the first time in paperback), and sometimes even commission them. Many originals are what are known as "category books" – westerns, romances, science fiction and non-fiction books on popular but specialist subjects such as gardening or home crafts. If you sell your book direct to a paperback house, you will receive a smaller royalty in most cases than you would from a hard cover publisher, but of course you will not have to split it as you would if the hardcover publisher had sold the book to the paperback house and then taken his share.

When a paperback publisher buys an original he will expect to control many of the subsidiary rights, just as a hardcover publisher would, and in recent years this side of the paperback business has expanded and become effective. Included among those rights would be that of licensing a hardcover edition, and this kind of reverse partnership between hard and soft cover has worked in a number of cases. If that kind of deal is made, the paperback publisher takes a share of the hardcover income, but it is usually a much smaller percentage than that of the paperback income taken by the hardcover house when the sale has been made in the more conventional way. Of course, the sums are usually very much smaller too.

There is, however, one very major problem facing the author who hopes to sell direct to a paperback publisher, and that is that the paperback houses (of which, remember, there are comparatively few) tend to be bestseller orientated. This means not only that they put almost all their efforts behind one or two "lead" titles every month, but also that if they have on their list a bestselling author who is also prolific, they are likely to keep a large number of his titles in print and this inevitably diminishes their appetite for less well-known authors. It also of course makes it much more difficult for the unknown book to find shelf space in the shops, and the display of a book and hence its immediate availability to the impulse buyer are essential in the paperback market; if a whole row of spaces in a rack of paperbacks is occupied by that bestselling author, it is very nice for him, but it doesn't leave much room for you. Paperback editors are well aware of this problem, and often try to encourage and introduce less well-known writers, but are sometimes hampered in this by their customers, the wholesalers, who will order the bestsellers in huge quantities, but may refuse to take even a token number of the book with a less familiar title and author's name. Even Penguin, for years able to publish books not aimed at the most popular end of the market, has been forced more recently to look for shorter-term sales and to compete more vigorously in the field of popular bestsellers with its more commercially orientated competitors.

Bookclubs

Bookclubs sell by direct mail, offering hardcover books at less than the normal price, which they achieve by purchasing copies from the publisher at high discounts, reducing the author's royalty, and by binding their members to the purchase of a given number of books per year. This commitment, though the member's obligation is usually no more than the purchase of one book every quarter, gives the club a captive market. At regular intervals the club's latest "choice" is sent and billed automatically to the members, unless they return a form saying that they do not wish to receive it; undoubtedly many copies of the choice are sold by this method to members who do not really want the book, but are too lazy or forgetful to return the form rejecting it.

The quantities of books that bookclubs take vary from one or two hundred to tens of thousands. Booksellers abhor the clubs, especially when they offer new members the introductory opportunity of buying expensive books for a ridiculously low price, at the same time as the bookseller is trying to sell the same title at full price. Publishers, on the other hand, welcome a bookclub order, since it is usually given before the book is printed, and can thus increase the print order and spread the origination cost of the book. Sometimes bookclubs print their own editions of books, and this affects the author since he will probably receive a slightly higher royalty on these copies than he does when the publisher supplies the bookclub with copies from his own stock; the bookclub is unlikely to print its own edition unless it is expecting to dispose of very large quantities of the book.

Bookclubs are highly competitive with each other, and prefer to have exclusivity on the books that they offer to their members, but increasingly, if the book has wide appeal, it is possible to sell rights to more than one club. After a bleak period in the 1960s, bookclubs are presently booming, and in addition to those which take a very wide range of books of general interest, there are now many specialist bookclubs devoted to one particular subject, such as cookery, ancient history, religion, and so on.

Condensed Books

Condensed books, mostly fiction, are sold by direct mail to subscribers. The shortening of his book may be a salutary experience for the author, demonstrating to him just how much of his original version was unnecessary verbiage; it may also cause him considerable pain at the disappearance of his fine writing and possibly the total elimination of scenes and characters which he considers essential to his story. The condensations are, however, done with considerable skill and as much sympathy as possible by the experienced editors employed by the condensed book publisher, and if the author is upset by what they do, his best course is to console himself with the cheque that he will receive for these rights.

Serial Rights

Very few books are serialized in their entirety nowadays, and it is usually a matter of an abridgement or extracts appearing in newspapers or magazines. First serial rights refer to such versions published prior to the publication of the book in volume form, while second serials are those published after publication in volume form. It is worth remembering that the market for serials is not confined to British newspapers and magazines, but extends to overseas journals too. The choice of extract or the abridgement is the responsibility of the newspaper or magazine which buys the rights. Serial rights are not necessarily exclusive, and the same book may achieve more than one sale in this area. Many writers, especially if their forte is romantic fiction, prepare their work first for the serial market, expanding it thereafter to book length for publication in volume form.

Foreign Rights

Translation rights can be very lucrative, despite the fact that the foreign publisher usually pays a lower rate of royalties (allowing him to include the cost of the translation in his budget without inflating the retail price). Let me repeat, sales of your original publisher's English language edition of your book in foreign countries do not come under Foreign rights, which are translation rights, sold to a foreign publisher who will bring out an edition of the book translated into his own language, whereas sales of the English language edition in foreign-speaking countries are export sales. It is customary for the foreign publisher to agree to publish a faithful translation of the book, and it should not be altered in any material way without your prior consent. You may well find, however, that minor changes have been made. In theory, the author should be consulted about all alterations, but in practice it is probably better to accept them with a good grace after the event, provided of course that they have not damaged your work, and enjoy the financial rewards. The foreign publisher will usually be granted volume rights in the book, and may therefore achieve for you a sale of the foreign language edition to paperback houses, bookclubs, magazines and so on in his country.

US Rights

If your book is sold to an American publisher, the contract will be basically similar to the agreement you sign with a British publisher, and will grant him much the same rights. It will almost certainly be a much longer document and may also be very much tougher on the author than most British publishing contracts. You should never, of course, sign any document without reading it carefully and understanding not only its benefits to you but your obligations under it and the restrictions it may place upon you, and care may be particularly necessary with American contracts. Royalties tend to be a little lower in the States than in Britain, but the quantities of books sold are often higher. If your book is lavishly illustrated, particularly if colour printing is involved, or if it is a somewhat elaborate production, it is quite likely that the British publisher will arrange to sell sheets of his edition to the American publisher who will buy them at a price only slightly above cost and inclusive of royalty. Your share will then be a percentage of the price received by the British publisher, and this is generally a ludicrously small amount in comparison with what you would receive if you were given a normal royalty on the American retail price of the book. It seems very unfair, but the economics of this kind of publishing really do not allow of a better deal for the author, and it is a question of accepting this small reward or getting nothing at all. All moneys due from a US publisher (and the same applies to Foreign language publishers) will be paid to your British publisher or to your agent, and of course their shares of the income will be deducted before it is passed on to you.

If you sign a contract directly with an American publisher (or with a foreign language publisher) you will become liable for income tax in the United States (or in the foreign language country) unless you apply specially for exemption on the grounds that you pay your taxes in your country of residence. A large number of countries has reciprocal double tax exemption arrangements with Britain. The Society of Authors, the Writers' Guild, your agent or your bank manager or accountant would be able to advise you.

Film Rights

If you are lucky, your book may sell to a film producer or company. The moneys involved are sometimes supplemented by a share of profits on the film, which is fine if the term used is "gross profits", but rather less exciting if the share is of "net profits", since in the film industry net profits sometimes disappear altogether, even on the most successful films. Better deals are for a share of net or gross receipts. What happens most often with film rights is that an option is purchased for a comparatively small sum, and such options have a habit of lapsing without the film being made. There is nothing to be done about this except to be grateful that you received a sum of money for nothing.

Dramatization, Radio and Television Rights

There is nothing special to note about these rights, except that there are two kinds of radio and television rights: those for a straight reading of the book (which is obviously more likely to occur on radio than on television) and those for a dramatization of it. Any abridgement or adaptation is undertaken by the radio or television company.

Anthology Rights

These do not apply only to true anthologies of poetry or prose, but also cover the granting of rights to other authors to use extracts from your work. If you are quoting from another person's work you must obtain permission to do so, and pay a fee for the privilege. Under rules known as "Fair Dealing" a limited amount from an author's work may be quoted without payment for purposes of criticism or review, but exactly how much may be used in this way is always a vexed question. It is always as well to apply in writing for permission to use someone else's material, approaching the publisher of the work and giving details of the use you intend to make of the quotation. The publisher will tell you in what form the obligatory acknowledgement of the source should be made and what fee, varying from nothing to large sums for a lengthy quote from an author of note, will be payable. It may seem a chore to have to do this and you may resent having to make the payment, but the boot will be on the other foot when others want to quote from you. For poets and short story writers in particular Anthology Rights can often provide a substantial income.

Large Print Rights

These are not always separately mentioned in contracts, since they can be covered under the publisher's right to license other hardcover editions of the book, but since more and more large print books are being published, some firms are including a separate clause in the contract to deal with them. Large print books are usually straightforward reprints of the original text, but set in a large size of type so that they can be read by the partially sighted. The specialist publishers of these editions pay royalties in the normal way. On the other hand, it is customary when a request is received to translate a book into Braille to grant permission without fee for either author or publisher.

Other Rights

There seems to be no end to the things that can happen to a book, and many publishers try to cover as many possibilities as they can in a subsidiary rights clause which refers to the use of the book for strip cartoons, for cassette or other recording, for micro-photographic reproduction, film-strip, and so on. Mechanical reproduction and video recording rights are growing in importance, and will continue to do so, to such an extent that in the future they, and other of these miscellaneous sub-rights, will probably be accorded separate sub-clauses in publishing contracts, rather than being lumped together as at present in a ragbag clause which suggests that they are of minor significance only.

Packagers

Packagers are people who conceive and produce books for regular publishers to sell. Thus they do all the work of the ordinary publisher up to the marketing, publicizing, selling and distribution of the work. Very often the books are fully illustrated, with a considerable amount of colour work, and the packager's aim is to sell the book not just to a British publisher, but simultaneously to an American house and to foreign language publishers as well; if he sells foreign language editions, he will have to print the black plate which includes the text separately, but he will be able to print the colour for all the editions at one time, which will be much more economical than printing them separately, and since he can put several publishers' print quantities together, he can arrive at a total print run large enough to reduce all his origination costs to a very reasonable sum per copy. Having had an idea for a book, a packager usually commissions an author to write it, paying him a lump sum according to the number of copies printed, or in some cases making a handsome outright payment, or paying a substantial advance on account of a modest royalty on net receipts. The author might stand to gain more if he received normal royalties from all the publishers concerned, but any shortfall in this direction is made up for by the fact that he receives his money in advance, before the books have been sold into the shops, since the publisher will have paid the packager a sum inclusive of royalties to cover all the copies he has ordered. As a matter of principle any author who is asked by a packager to write a book should aim to get some kind of royalty. After all, packaged books are often very successful, and get reprinted.

Sponsored Books

Sponsored books used to consist almost entirely of histories of large businesses, produced to celebrate some anniversary, paid for out of the firm's advertising budget, and distributed to the staff and customers. Such books were not usually on sale to the general public. Nowadays, however, many large organizations see the sponsoring of books, whether or not their subject is directly connected with the interest of the organization, as a useful kind of publicity. The books are usually published by a hardcover house in the normal way, the only real difference being that all or a proportion of the costs are paid by the sponsor, who often takes a share of the profits on the books, if any. Some sponsors have retailing facilities available or are prepared to spend considerable sums in publicizing the book, and this may result in an abnormally large print quantity being ordered. That is very pleasant for the author, though there are some cases where the sponsors will try to buy the author's copyright for an outright sum, and even if the amount is generous, the author may suffer from this arrangement. Or they may propose a low royalty, pleading the need to keep the retail price down and explaining that the author will still be well paid since the high sales envisaged should compensate him for earning less than the norm on each copy. You can of course try a little bargaining.

Vanity Publishing

Some authors who cannot secure commercial publication for their books, or who are merely taken in by attractive advertisements, pay to have their work published. If you want to do this, go ahead. It's your money, and you're entitled to do what you like with it. Don't expect, however, to see many copies of the book – it certainly isn't likely to appear in bookshops – and don't expect to see your money back, whatever the agreement you sign may say about the royalties that you will collect on the vast sales the vanity publishers predict. They won't materialize. Vanity publishers take your money and give your ego a boost that you could probably find much more cheaply in a bottle of liquor or a new dress or whatever turns you on. Occasionally some respectable publishing houses will make an arrangement with an author for him to subsidize publication of his book in some way, but in such cases the contract normally provides, or should provide, that the author will receive his money back, plus royalties, once the book has achieved a certain level of sales and the publisher's risk has been minimized. In general, you should not have to pay to have a book published – the publisher should pay you.

If you must see your work in print and you cannot find a regular publisher to take you on, then rather than go to a vanity publisher, your best bet is to contact a reputable printer who will produce it for you. You will have only his costs and profit to pay for. Admittedly, you will then have to arrange for your own distribution, but by selling copies to your friends and perhaps persuading your local bookseller to display the book (you will probably have to supply him "on sale or return", so that he will only pay you when he has actually sold the book, and of course he will take a discount of at least a third on the sale) you are still likely to do as well as if you went to a vanity house.

Copyright

Unless there are very special reasons for so doing, you should never surrender the copyright to your books. Copyright means, of course, that no one has the right to print, publish or sell any work or part thereof without the permission of the copyright holder, who is normally, in the case of books, the author. There are some circumstances in which a publisher may wish to buy the copyright in your work, usually offering an outright fee. Since the fee is frequently a sum larger than the author might expect to receive simply as an advance against royalties, he may be tempted to accept it. But he should think carefully before doing so. Once he has parted with the copyright, the publisher will be able to go on producing the work, possibly in very large quantities, without paying the author any additional money, and the outright sum he received may end up looking very small against the royalties that the work's sale would have brought in, even if those royalties had been on a low scale. And if the publisher has bought the copyright in your book he is free to edit it, change it, abridge it, and indeed do anything he likes with it, without consulting you or paying you any more money, no matter how much it may earn for him. Parting with your copyright is not only foolish, but normally pretty irreversible – even if the firm to which you have sold it goes out of existence you are unlikely to get your copyright back.

Your book is protected by copyright as soon as it is written, but it is useful to establish the date of its completion, which you can do, for instance, by depositing a copy of it with your bank and obtaining a dated receipt. On publication, the printing in the book of the symbol ©, the name of the copyright owner and the date of first publication secures protection in all countries which are signatories to the Universal Copyright Convention, numbering over sixty nations throughout the world. Some books do get pirated – that is to say they are published without authorization, and without payment, during the period of copyright in certain parts of the world. If you learn of the pirating of one of your books, inform your agent and/or your publisher or, if you are a member, the Society of Authors or the Writers' Guild, and do so immediately. The same advice applies if you discover that your work has been plagiarized or that your copyright has been infringed in any other way. Incidentally, before rushing too precipitately into action, you should bear in mind that while a direct quotation of your words may be a clear-cut case of plagiarism, it is rather more difficult to prove that similarities of plot have been pinched by one writer from another.

Copyright in a work published during the author's lifetime extends for fifty years after the author's death, and this applies in most countries of the world, though in some the term is shorter and in others longer. When you die your copyrights become part of your estate, and unless you leave them in your will to a specific person, will pass to your residual legatee. As assets, they may be liable to tax, and your publisher or agent will be asked to place a value on them so that the Capital Taxes Office can make the necessary assessment.

There is no copyright in titles, nor in ideas. However, if you publish a book called, say, *The Day of the Jackal*, you could be sued for "passing off" (i.e. hoping to make people buy your book by giving them the impression that it is Frederick Forsyth's famous bestseller), and if you follow too closely the plot of an already published book or copy parts of it without permission and giving the impression that they are your own work, you can be sued for plagiarism.

Translators

When a publisher buys the rights to a foreign language book, it is he who hires a translator to render it into his own language. Usually he will commission the translation on an outright basis, paying the translator an agreed flat sum per thousand words, but in some cases (and the Translators Association of the Society of Authors would advise this) it is possible for the translator to receive a royalty, particularly if the work concerned is out of copyright, so that the publisher has no royalties to pay to the author. English language publishers quite often receive requests for permission to translate books from the publishers' lists into foreign languages; the reply is always that that is the concern of a foreign publisher, that no such permission is likely to be given until a foreign language publisher has bought the rights for that particular language, and that he will then probably commission a translator who is already known to him to do the job.

The Net Book Agreement

Some years ago, after the introduction of the Restrictive Practices Act of 1956, which followed a Monopolies Commission investigation into restrictive practices, the British Publishers Association fought a long battle in the Restrictive Practices Court over the question of whether it was in the public interest not to allow retail outlets to price books at their own discretion, but to maintain the arrangement of the Net Book Agreement, which had for many years ensured that the publisher fixed the retail price and the bookshops maintained it. The Act contained a number of tests designed to protect the public against restrictions on free competition. The Court had to consider the arguments in favour of competition and the arguments for allowing the market to fix its own prices, and was finally won over by the Publishers Association's arguments and the Net Book Agreement is still with us. In certain parts of the world, however, retail price maintenance for books has been abandoned; when this happens, as it did in Australia, it is amid cries of woe and doom. However, the Australian book trade seems so far to have survived.

Perhaps we shall eventually see the disappearance of the Net Book Agreement in Britain, but let us hope that we never see the imposition of VAT or any similar tax on books. We were saved from this back in 1940 when the then Chancellor of the Exchequer, Kingsley Wood, was about to introduce Purchase Tax. A strong campaign was mounted by authors and publishers, spearheaded by Stanley Unwin, who, in a celebrated letter to *The Times* argued that a tax on books was a tax on knowledge. His letter continued, "It would be humiliating if, in a war for freedom of thought, the sale of books in which man's highest thoughts are enshrined should be hampered by taxation." The Chancellor eventually gave in, but few other countries have been able similarly to escape.

Editorial Titles

Some editors are called simply "editors", while others have elaborate titles which may be very confusing. Such titles have proliferated in recent years, partly as a result of periods of wage restraint, when the only way to give someone a pay rise was to invent a new title for him as justification for a change of salary, and partly because of union insistence on job definition and differentiation. The titles used and the responsibilities of their bearers differ from company to company. There are two main editorial functions: one is the acquisition of new books, and the other the checking and preparation of authors' typescripts before they are sent to the printer. The functions may overlap, or both may be performed by the same person. In general, the former have titles such as "Acquiring Editor" or "Commissioning Editor" or "Sponsoring Editor", whereas the latter are more likely to be called "Copy Editor" or "House Editor". Some acquiring editors may use a title referring to the section of the list which they handle, such as "Science Editor" or "Children's Books Editor". Many editorial titles are used only within the publishing house, and as far as the outside world and the author is concerned, the designation will often be restricted to "Editorial Director", "Senior Editor", "Managing Editor" (if used accurately, this title should suggest that its bearer is the person who allocates editorial work, whether acquisitional or copy-editing, among the personnel in the editorial department) or plain "Editor". If the title and the responsibilities of the person with whom you are dealing are not clear to you, then it is worth asking. It is always easier to work with someone if you know what he does and what he does not do. Moreover, your editor will probably enjoy explaining it all to you – most people respond readily when someone shows interest in the details of their work.

2

Submitting Your Work to a Publisher

Preparation of the Typescript

Handwriting was all very well for Jane Austen, but nowadays few publishers would be prepared to consider a manuscript (using that term in its true meaning of material written by hand). A typescript is required (even if it is often loosely and perversely referred to as a "manuscript"), and it should be in double spacing on one side of the paper only, with margins on both edges of the paper. Why is this important? First of all, because your material will be easier to read. Double spacing will also allow room for corrections which do not warrant retyping. Margins at the sides will permit the compositor (the person who puts the book into type) to put each page into a kind of stand which has grips on either side to hold it in place while he copies it.

There are different rules for the layout of poetry and plays. Poems should be typed exactly as they are intended to appear in print, in single spacing with any indentations or other singularities just as you want them. Plays demand special and complex layouts, advice on which can be obtained from play publishers or from the BBC Radio Drama department, which has a useful leaflet on the subject.

The paper used should not be smaller than Quarto. A4 is currently very popular, but if you are submitting a typescript direct to an American publisher he will probably prefer to have it on Quarto. Do your best to keep to the same number and width of lines per page, and if you use more than one typewriter it is preferable that they should all have the same size of type – these considerations making it much easier to work out the length of the book, quite apart from the fact that the typescript will look neater.

Many authors tend to economize on typewriter ribbons. It doesn't help. Why put an obstacle in the way of your book by making it physically difficult for the publisher to read? Equally, masses of messy corrections are to be avoided. That doesn't mean that you can't make the occasional alteration, but the cleaner the typescript looks the better. If you do make a correction, make sure that the change is totally clear, and if it is of any length or complexity, retype the page.

You should make at least two carbon copies of your typescript. When submitting a book, always send the top copy to a publisher rather than a carbon. If he decides to take the book on, he will probably want a second copy, and your first carbon copy will be acceptable. The second carbon copy is for yourself, and you should retain it with the utmost care. You may want to refer to it in working with your publisher, and you will certainly need it if the other copies are lost or damaged. Typescripts sometimes go astray in the post or are mislaid in the most scrupulously monitored of publisher's offices (and not all are that!) or can be damaged by fire or flood, and if any such disaster should take place, it is much easier to have the book retyped or photocopied from your own carbon than to have to start writing it again from scratch. Photocopying is just as acceptable, if not more so, than carbon copying, if you can afford it. If you are using carbons, again don't indulge in false economy, but replace the carbons as soon as the copies begin to look grey.

The pages of your typescript should be numbered consecutively from the first page to the last, not starting from "1" again at the beginning of each new chapter. If you have ever dropped a typescript of separate pages and tried to put it in order again, you will appreciate how much more difficult a task it would be if the chapters were each numbered separately. Put "The End" at the end, even if you don't want it to appear in the final printed version; endings are sometimes inconclusive, but if "The End" is there the publisher will know that that is where you intended to stop.

Publishers vary in their likes and dislikes about how a typescript should be fastened together. The universally unpopular method is that in which the pages are bound solidly together, which makes the book impossibly heavy and awkward to read. Looseleaf binders are often used; the ring variety is not too bad, but pages frequently slip out of the sort which relies on some kind of spring to keep them in place. Paperclips should be avoided, if only because other pieces of paper so easily get caught up in them. My own preference in my days as a publisher was for entirely loose leafs, the typescript either contained in the box the paper came in or secured with rubber bands. However, stapling is acceptable, either in chapters or in batches of a regular number of pages, but only one staple, at the top left-hand corner, is needed.

How long should a book be? A glib, but nevertheless true answer is that it should be as long as it needs to be. If you set out to write, say, eighty thousand words, you may find that you have to pad your material or conversely to condense it. Let the book find its own length. There are no rules – very short and very long books do get published – but there are guidelines. In most cases, publishers do not want anything much under thirty-five thousand words (except for children's books) and tend to look apprehensively at anything which runs to more than a hundred thousand words. If you can keep to somewhere between fifty and eighty thousand words you will probably stand more chance. But, as I have already said, there are no hard and fast rules. British publishers with an eye on the American market may well accept a very long novel, since American publishers seem currently to be seeking for such books. On the other hand, if you are writing for a series, you may have to stick closely to a length decided in advance by the publisher.

How many chapters should your book have? Again, there are no rules. Some books have no chapters, and others are broken into hundreds of short sections. If you come to a "natural break" in your narrative, then you have probably come to the end of a chapter. But I doubt if any books have ever been turned down for having either too few or too many chapters.

It is not absolutely necessary to indicate on the front page of your typescript how many words it contains, since most publishers are practised at gauging the length of the books they receive, but it does no harm to show the extent, and indeed it may be a help. The publishers of this book, Robert Hale Limited, issue an excellent guide to the calculation of the length of a typescript and, with their permission, I shall now quote it:

> The purpose of calculating the wordage of any typescript is to determine the number of printed pages it will occupy. The precise word count is of no use, since it tells nothing about the matter of short lines resulting from paragraphing or dialogue (particularly important with fiction).
>
> Calculation is therefore based on the assumption that all

printed pages have no paragraph beginnings or endings and the type area is completely filled with words.

To assess the wordage proceed as follows:

1. Ensure the typewriting is the same throughout in terms of size, length of line etc. If not the procedure given below should be followed separately for each individual style of typing and the results added together.
2. Count 50 full-length lines and find the average number of words, e.g. 50 lines of 560 words gives an average of 11.2 words.
3. Average the number of lines over 10 characteristic pages, e.g. 245 lines on 10 pages gives an average of 24.5 lines.
4. Multiply the averages of 2. and 3. to get average per page, e.g. $11.2 \times 24.5 = 274$.
5. Ensure the page numbering is consecutive, then multiply the word average per page by the number of pages (count short pages at beginnings and ends of chapters as full pages).
6. Draw attention to, but do not count, foreword, preface, introduction, bibliography, appendices, index, maps or other line figures.

Some authors are in the habit of putting "First British Serial Rights" on the front page of their typescripts, in the mistaken belief that this is what they are offering to the publisher. They should be offering him volume rights, or at least British volume rights, or possibly all rights. First British Serial Rights are what you offer to a magazine or newspaper if you submit your book to them before or instead of showing it to a book publisher.

Do put your name and address on the title-page and last page of your typescript.

Words are the main tool of the author's trade, and they should be correctly used and spelt and punctuated. I have always considered that failure in these respects is the sign of an unprofessional approach. I do recognize that some writers have an impenetrable blindspot in certain of these matters, particularly spelling, and that even the most careful scrutiny of dictionaries and grammars cannot entirely solve their problems. In which case, I would suggest that before finally typing their books, or at least before submitting them if they are already typed, they should prevail upon a friend with the right capabilities to go through the books and make the necessary alterations. Such glamour attaches to authorship, that it should not be difficult to find a friend who will undertake this chore. Teachers are very suitable, though it is as well to choose one who has retired or is at least elderly – the younger ones may be as hopeless as you yourself.

Sending the Book Out

Having got your typescript ready, in the best possible condition that you can manage, where do you send it? In *The Writers' and Artists' Year Book* you will find a list of publishers and their addresses. Some indication of the kinds of books that each firm publishes is given, but the information is often too brief and general to be more than the roughest of guides. Rather than using a pin to decide which publisher you will try, it is a good idea to visit your local bookshop and library and see which companies regularly produce books of the kind which you have written. It may be stating the obvious, but it is of little use to send, say, a romantic novel to a publisher who produces nothing but school text books, or an art book to a publisher who never ventures into that field. On the other hand, you should beware of working too closely on what you discover in the bookshop; if you have written, say, a new biography of Mary, Queen of Scots, it is probably a waste of time and money to send it to a publisher who has recently brought out a book on the very same subject, or who has a standard work on it on his backlist; try another house which has a list of biographies.

When you have selected your publisher you can simply send your typescript to him. In these days of very high postal costs for parcels it is, however, wiser to write first asking if you may submit the book. Tell the publisher, briefly, what it is about. If it is a novel, specify what genre it is ("straight", romantic, thriller, detective, western, etc), or if it is non-fiction, give a few details of your qualifications for writing it and possibly something about the market for which it is intended. You will have little chance of getting that biography of Mary, Queen of Scots published unless you are an accredited historian or have had access to new, unpublished material about her (though of course there are always exceptions to a statement of that sort – if you are a well-known writer, or have not found new material but a really new angle, or if you write so well that you have brought the lady to life as no one else ever has, for instance).

Do not tell the publisher that all your friends have enjoyed the book. He won't be impressed, partly because he does not know your friends and so has no idea whether or not he can respect their judgement, and partly because he will suspect that your friends will have told you that they enjoyed it even if in fact they loathed every word. On the other hand, if you happen to have had an endorsement from some eminent personage, especially if he is in the field in which you are writing, by all means say so. Equally, if you are writing, for instance, a book on safety in the home and have shown it to an organization such as RoSPA, who have given it their approval, say so. Or if the book is aimed at a specialist market, it will probably be worthwhile to give some details of the numbers of people likely to be keenly interested in the book.

Over the years I spent in publishing I received thousands of letters about books which the authors wished me to consider. Some were grovelling ("I would consider it an honour to be published by such a great firm as yours"), some were overbearing ("I have decided that you should publish this book. Kindly state your terms by return"), some were jokey ("My Mum thinks it's smashing, but I do recognize that she may be a teeny bit prejudiced in my favour"), some were apologetic and often tended to misquote ("A poor thing but my own"), some were so long that I felt I didn't need to read the book itself, and some were so illiterate that I knew I didn't have to. The ones I liked best were brief and to the point, businesslike, professional.

Send a stamped addressed envelope with your letter of enquiry. You may feel that the publisher should well be able to afford to pay for the postage on his letter back to you, but you should remember that you are in a buyer's market, and don't ask him to spend money on something which may not interest him.

It may be worth your while to find out the editor's name so that you can address your letter to him personally (not that, if it is a large editorial department, he will necessarily be the person to read it). If you do so, however, make sure that you get the name right. Some people are very sensitive about misspellings of their name (personally, I am inured to it after long experience) or to being addressed as "Ms" when in fact they are "Mr" or "Mrs" or even old-fashioned "Miss".

If the publisher says that he is willing to consider the book, then post it to him, or deliver it if you are near enough to his office. Enclose postage for its return. Don't, if you deliver it, expect to see anyone in the office – at that stage no one is interested in you. Your book is your ambassador. And if you feel that you have to see someone to explain about the book, then there is probably something wrong with it. Your book should speak for itself. After all, you aren't going to be able to stand in bookshops explaining it to potential customers, are you?

When you send your book to a publisher you should receive an acknowledgement of its arrival. If you do not receive such an acknowledgement it may mean that the parcel has been lost in the mail, or it may be simply that the publisher has decided to economize by not sending out those expensive (cost of stationery, secretary's time, postage) pieces of paper. Some authors enclose a stamped addressed postcard which the publisher can send off when the parcel arrives. It is all an additional expense for the author, but like paper, typewriter ribbons, carbons, and of course time and hard work, it is simply an investment that he has to make.

Synopses and Specimen Chapters

Instead of sending the complete book, you can send a specimen chapter or two and a synopsis. In my opinion, that is rarely a good idea, unless you are already known to the publisher. The best of synopses and specimen chapters cannot give an entirely reliable picture of the book as a whole, especially if it is fiction. When I was a publisher and was sent such a submission, I usually replied, if I were interested, asking for the completed work to be sent to me in due course, but without making any commitment. "Well," you may say, "I don't want to waste my time writing a full-length book if it's not going to be accepted." I understand that, but alas it's what a new author has to do. Commissions on part of the material are rarely given to untried authors.

Naturally, there are exceptions. If an author writes to a publisher with an idea for a book (particularly in the non-fiction field), describing it in some detail, giving his own qualifications for writing it, and perhaps even some information about the potential market, the publisher might ask him to submit a full synopsis and some specimen chapters, and on that basis, almost certainly with the addition of meetings and discussions between publisher and author, the book might be commissioned. Or, if you happen to be an expert in a particular field, the first approach may come from a publisher, inviting you to write a given book, in which case he might again ask for a synopsis and specimen chapters just to make sure that you are really capable of doing the work.

If you are commissioned to write a book on the basis of a synopsis, you do not have to stick to it absolutely rigidly. Obviously, you must do your best to deliver the book that the publisher expects, but minor differences from the original synopsis will not worry your publisher too much. He is used to the fact that authors change their ideas sometimes in the course of writing, or find that something which sounds perfectly fine in brief will not work properly when it is expanded. If the changes are at all major, you should of course let your publisher know about them in advance, especially if they alter the scope of the book in some way.

Many established writers produce all of their books "on spec" – that is to say, without a contract until the book has been finished and accepted for publication. Others are fortunate enough to be commissioned for each of their books, but in those cases, even though the author is very experienced and trustworthy, the publisher may ask him for a detailed synopsis. The main use of this will be for the editor to show to other people. For him, the title and your name may be sufficient. For others, both inside and outside his own publishing house, more details may well be useful.

Even less to be recommended than the synopsis and specimen chapter as a first approach is the submission which takes the form of two or three pages, taken apparently at random from a book. Intended to whet the publisher's appetite, such submissions are merely irritating and a complete waste of time and postage.

Agents

You may decide instead of submitting your work directly to a publisher to send it first to an agent, and in many ways this can be a very wise move. The advantages of using an agent are many: he knows the state of the market much better than you are likely to, for he is in regular touch with all the principal publishers and is aware of the kinds of books they are looking for at any given juncture; he sends the book out at his own expense; he will negotiate the contract with the publisher, getting the best possible deal for his author, ensuring that the latter's rights are always preserved, and can often help to keep the publisher up to scratch, so that the book is handled well in every aspect; he collects any moneys due, and checks that they are correct; he will undertake the sale of many of the subsidiary rights; and, one of the agent's most important functions, he will stand between the author and the publisher in the case of any dispute, enabling the author to remain on friendly terms with his publisher despite the fact that, through the agent, they may be at loggerheads; he may also well be able to save you from having the dispute in the first place, for though he is your representative and therefore on your side, he does also have a wide experience of publishers and their problems (indeed, many agents have spent part of their careers as publishers) and may therefore be able to explain things that you don't understand, and tell you whether your complaint is justified or not; he will also probably be able to give you some advice about tax on your earnings as an author; and he will often give useful editorial advice on a typescript.

For all these services, the agent will normally charge the author 10 per cent of his earnings from the book, plus VAT, though he may take a higher percentage on foreign earnings. The higher rate on foreign earnings comes about because the British agent has made the foreign sale through a foreign agent who represents him in the country concerned. The foreign agent takes his cut on the moneys earned in that country, and transmits the balance to the British agent, who takes his percentage before passing it on to the author. Some authors resent having to pay a double commission in this way, and in certain circumstances their feelings may be justified. It is obviously a matter to be discussed directly with the agent.

Good agents do not charge for reading typescripts submitted to them by potential new clients, though it would not be surprising if this became normal practice, nor, if they take you on to their list of clients, do they take their percentage until they have sold your book and the money comes in. The agent's cut is usually (though not always) well earned, and any totally inexperienced author would be well advised to go to an agent. That is, if he can find one who is willing to act for him, which may not be easy. Agents are almost as difficult to find as publishers. Not unreasonably, they tend not to take on an author unless they are convinced that within a reasonable period they will be making enough money from him to cover their costs, their overheads and a profit. If an agent takes you on to his books he is undoubtedly hoping that within two or three years you will be earning upwards of £5,000 a year, and therefore contributing £500 a year to his coffers.

If you experience difficulty in finding an agent to take you on, and as already suggested it may be difficult at an early stage in your writing career, your best bet may be to try one of the newer, smaller agencies. You may not be getting quite the same expertise and experience, but the new agent's enthusiasm and need to establish himself may work to your benefit.

Agents cannot of course perform miracles. If you get an agent to act for you, it does not necessarily mean that he will be able to sell all your ideas or completed books. Nor, though he may try to help his clients, is he usually in the business of teaching incompetent writers how to write. And though again, in very special circumstances, he may occasionally subsidize an author in a minor way, he is not, any more than your publisher is, in the banking business, and neither an agent nor a publisher should be expected to advance money to authors other than under the terms of a contract.

Naturally, agents vary in their competence. You may find after a while that you are dissatisfied with yours. There is nothing to stop you changing to another agent if you can find one to take you on. However, you should give the first agent notice of your intention to change, and he is entitled to continue to act for you and to take his commission in respect of any books which he has handled for you, provided the original contract he negotiated has not been terminated.

Waiting for the Result of a Submission

Having submitted your book to a publisher, how long can you expect to wait before receiving a verdict? Anything between two and eight weeks, and often longer. Some publishers are remarkably dilatory in this respect, and one frequently hears stories of books kept for a year or more before a decision is made. If the publisher has kept in touch with the author during that time to explain why it is taking him so long, the author may have less cause for complaint, but in most such cases, the author hears nothing. This seems to me to be quite outrageous. It can happen to experienced writers too. A friend of mine, with over fifty successful books to her credit, recently submitted an idea to two publishers (not simultaneously – one after the other). She sent a brief synopsis of the book, a description of the market envisaged, details of her own qualifications and of the research that she had already done and the offers of help and support for the eventual book that she had received from organizations in the field which the book covered. This very professionally presented material, which is halfway, as it were, between a letter of enquiry and a full synopsis, would take at most a quarter of an hour to read. Of course, time would be needed to discuss the idea with other members of the publishing house and perhaps to investigate the market – perhaps two weeks, one might think. The first firm acknowledged receipt of the material by return but then kept it for six weeks before rejecting it; the second publisher did not acknowledge receipt and, at the time of writing, has had it for seven weeks without response.

Sometimes publishers return books almost immediately upon receipt. This does not necessarily mean that your work has not been seriously considered, though it may be simply that you chose a publisher who was not interested at that juncture in the kind of book you had written. Often, however, a speedy return indicates no more than that you were lucky enough to send your book in when there was not a great pile of typescripts on the editor's desk waiting to be read, so that he was able to give you prompt attention. Now, he may not have read the book all the way through, and may in fact have read only a few sentences. Don't feel hard done by. One thing that publishers are very good at is recognizing material that they do not want to publish. They may be making a terrible mistake in turning down your masterpiece so easily, but although most publishers can tell you of the bestsellers that they let slip through their fingers, most would also be able to say with truth that they rarely had reason to regret one of these hasty decisions. Even if they did regret it, they would console themselves with the thought that another interesting book would almost certainly happen along very shortly.

If your book does not come back immediately, it may be that it has spent most of its time in the publisher's office working its way from the bottom of the pile to the top. It isn't always a steady progression. Sometimes a book will arrive at the publisher's office and usurp your position in the queue because it is by one of the publisher's established authors, or because an agent has sent it in suggesting that it is a potential bestseller and asking for a speedy decision. Most publishers receive a very large number of typescripts for their consideration, and delays are inevitable.

It might be worth diverging at this point to comment on the widespread belief that publishers do not like direct submissions from authors, preferring to receive all submissions through agents. This is totally untrue, and indeed there are many publishers who greatly prefer to deal directly with authors and who look upon agents, or some of them, as enemies. What is true is that a publisher knows that a book which comes from an agent must have a modicum of merit, or the agent would not have agreed to handle it, and if the agent is one that he knows and trusts and the agent is very enthusiastic about the book, then he will undoubtedly give it special consideration. However, it is the book itself which will have to make the publisher enthusiastic, and that can happen whether it comes through an agent or directly from its author.

If your book does not come back from the publisher by return of post, you still may not have to wait long. It may be given a preliminary reading, perhaps by an outside reader, perhaps by a junior editor. If either of those persons feels that the book would not be of interest to his firm, then the typescript will come back to you soon thereafter. If, however, he finds it interesting, then a further reading will probably be arranged. Comparatively few books are taken by the publishers on the basis of one reading only, unless perhaps the book lands first of all on the desk of a director or a senior editor whose decision can be accepted without question. Even then, nowadays most publishers will prepare estimates in some detail before accepting a book, and this may take a considerable time, especially if the book is complicated (for instance, with diagrams to be inserted into the text, or numerous headings and subheadings and material to be set in different sizes of type, and so on).

Many books are rejected at the estimate stage. However enthusiastic the editor may have been, the publisher wants to see a profit on the book, and if the potential market for it is not large enough, then he will not be able to spread the costs of origination (that is to say, the setting of the book in print, the preparation of the jacket, and all the other costs which have to be borne before a single copy can be produced) so as to come to a retail price for the book which will not inhibit sales by being too high and which will still allow him to make his profit. A very few publishers are willing now and then to publish a book on which it is expected that they will make a loss – it might be a novel of exceptional literary merit, or perhaps poetry – but such instances are rare.

Perhaps this is an appropriate place to point out that when he commits himself to the publication of a book, the publisher is also, on average, committing himself to an expenditure in the region of £7,000, that being what it will cost him to pay the author his advance and produce an edition of a few thousand copies. The figure does not allow anything for his overheads, which will come out of the profits he makes if he sells sufficient quantities of the book to pass his break-even point. It is not surprising then that publishers check their figures with great care, and tend to take on only those books whose profitability they feel is certain.

Sometimes, before a decision is made, a hardcover publisher will submit a typescript which he is considering to a paperback publisher to see if he has a good chance of selling the paperback rights. Whether he is morally justified in doing so is far from certain – the author has shown him the book in confidence, as it were, and he has no right to let other parties see it unless the author has given him specific permission to do so. Nevertheless, the addition of some kind of income from paperback or other subsidiary rights is often the only factor which makes it possible for the hardcover publisher to take on a book which he does not expect to be able to sell himself in sufficient quantities to make his own edition self-supporting, and this, he would argue, is justification for trying to find the outside help he needs.

In view of the length of time that publishers frequently take to make a decision, many authors feel that they should make multiple submissions – that is to say, send copies of their book to more than one publisher simultaneously. Some publishers are beginning to accept this practice, but it will not endear you to the majority. It is true that agents sometimes submit a book to several publishers simultaneously and indeed conduct an auction, selling the rights to the highest bidder, or the one who combines a good offer with known abilities, but the books concerned are nearly always potential bestsellers and have usually already made a name for themselves in the American market. In such cases, the agents are for once in a strong seller's market, and when you are in that position you can afford to do things which would normally be unpopular.

So unless you are already an author of very high standing, you will probably have to suffer the delays. Do you suffer in silence? Yes, for perhaps three months, after which it would be reasonable to write to the publisher and enquire politely what is happening. Some publishers will already have let you know by that time that they are tentatively interested in the book and will have explained that there will be a further delay while they prepare estimates, but in many cases there will simply be silence. If when you write after three months, you still get no satisfaction, then you have chosen an inefficient publisher (and there are many of them around). There is not a great deal that you can effectively do. At the end of six months without a decision, it is time to get stroppy, and demand the return of your typescript. That may mean the end of your chances with that particular publisher, but if he has already proved lackadaisical, you will be better off elsewhere. Nothing of course can compensate you for the lost time, and since there is little in the law books about the time that a publisher takes to make a decision, there is nothing to be gained from consulting your solicitor.

It is possible that the delay in reaching a decision is occasioned by the fact that the publisher has lost your typescript, an unfortunate occurrence which he is reluctant to confess. It does happen, even in the best-run offices. Most acknowledgement forms which publishers send out contain a statement to the effect that they accept no responsibility for the loss or damage of a typescript while it is in their possession, and you will not automatically get compensation for the loss, unless you have taken out your own insurance, which is a wise thing to do if you can afford it. But at the worst, you should still have your second copy of the book, and you will eventually be able to start the process of submission all over again.

The Rejected Typescript

If your book is rejected it will probably come back to you with nothing more than a formal statement that the publisher does not wish to take the book on to his list. There a few publishers who take the trouble to explain briefly why they are turning a book down, but the majority do not, and I am not sure that you can expect it of them. It would of course be of immense value to you if the publisher told you what was wrong, but think of how many books he rejects every week – probably nine out of every ten scripts submitted to him – and then consider how much of that week he would spend, if he wrote in detail about the books he was rejecting, on books that he is not going to publish. If he does bother to write a letter explaining his decision, you may well take it as a hopeful sign – not that he is going to change his mind, but at least that he had found enough in your typescript to make him feel that it is worthwhile to take time to make the explanation. If, having received a formal rejection, you persist and write to ask why your book has been turned down, you may not even get a reply. This is not really as discourteous as it may sound. Many editors would like to correspond with the authors they reject, in an effort to help them, but they simply do not have the time. Looking after the books and their authors that they are going to publish leaves very few spare moments. Besides, they are paid to concern themselves with the interests of their employers, which do not include correspondence with re-jected authors. Don't even write if you get a helpful rejection letter, apart perhaps from saying "thank you", unless the editor has plainly invited you to do so. Don't waste time on what will be a fruitless exercise. Simply send your book off to another publisher.

How often should you submit a book before giving up? The answer depends on your patience and how much you are prepared to spend on postage, and possibly on retyping the book, which is bound to get slightly tatty after several read-ings and which may require updating. If you receive any kind of encouragement, despite the rejections, then it is certainly worth continuing to try. If you have received nothing but formal rejections, you should perhaps ask yourself, after the typescript has come back, say, six times, whether there is indeed something wrong with it. Of course you may find it quite impossible to see its failings, and friends are usually not much use in this respect, since they will rarely tell you the truth about the book if they don't think it's very good, for fear of hurting your feelings. If you put it away for a good long period – three months or more – you may find at the end of that time that you can judge it with better impartiality. On the other hand, you can just go on sending it out, hoping that one day it will find a home, and taking heart from the many stories of very successful authors who collected large numbers of rejection slips for their first book before finally placing it happily.

Your problem is to find someone in a publishing house somewhere who loves the book. Liking is not enough. You need an editor who is really enthusiastic, and who will if necessary fight his company to persuade them to take the book on. Some authors believe that you have little chance of publication unless you know someone in a publishing house. Knowing someone may get you rather more careful consideration than otherwise, but, believe me, you still won't get taken on unless that someone, or somebody else in the same house, loves your book. Keep trying. You can even try the same publisher more than once, after a decent interval, because publishing personnel change, and your book may land on the desk of a different editor from the one who saw it last time, and he may be the lover you're looking for. However, if you are going to send it to a publisher who has already rejected it once, you should probably not do so unless there was some kind of encouragement from him in the first rejection, and certainly not without indicating that it is a second submission.

3

What Are Publishers Looking For?

Primarily, these days, publishers are looking for books that will make money. In the good old days, when publishing was an occupation for gentlemen (nowadays, even if you feel that it is an occupation for incompetents, it is more accurately described as an occupation for business men), publishers were able to take an overall view, and if they had a bestseller on their list would be able to use some of the money that it made for them in publishing other books which were worthy but which would almost certainly make a loss. Provided that the year's results ended up in the black, it did not matter too much if you published, for instance, small volumes of poetry which might have been printed in red ink for all the contribution to the firm's profit that they would make. Admittedly, it was easier in those days; book prices were high in relation to the cost of production, overheads were low and so were taxes, and even a 25 per cent royalty, which was frequently paid on the higher sales of a bestseller, was not crippling to the publisher as it would be today. There were several other factors too which helped the pre-war publisher, such as his ability to bind only those copies of a book needed for fairly immediate sale, and the fact that he could dispose of his overstocks by reducing the retail price and still make a profit.

In recent years, accountants have increasingly dominated publishing. A few of them do understand what publishing is all about, including such concepts as undertaking the publication of unprofitable first novels in the belief that the author will ultimately become successful, but in many firms there is now an insistence that every single book must reach a fairly high level of profitability, and the editor's role has become subjugated to that of the money-man. It is a very unfortunate development.

Robin Denniston, Academic Publisher of the Oxford University Press, said recently in a paper given to a meeting of the

University, College and Research Section of the Library Association,

> There are, it is true, areas of publishing (from which I exclude trade and consumer magazines) where market considerations are almost totally dominant – pre-eminently in mass-market paperbacks. Even there, however, I say "almost", because I have noticed throughout a longish association with such firms that the person who *makes the difference* in any list, however trashy it might appear, is the editor, whose own interests, subliminal drives, ambitions and egos (often huge) dictate ultimately what is acquired, for how much, and consequently the degree of emphasis placed on each new book. The shape and above all the flavour of the list is determined, here as elsewhere, by the editorial publisher.
>
> This may sound revisionist, but I believe it is such an important concept in the working life of a publisher that it cannot be repeated often enough – and the day when, in any firm, the accountant or even the marketing department finally takes over as publisher is a bad day in the life of that firm – bad not immediately and not purely in the quality of the list – bad, ultimately, for the profitability and well-being of that firm.

Mr Denniston is perhaps generalizing a little too freely – I am sure he would agree, as I have already said, that there are some accountants in the publishing trade whose attitude is liberal and enlightened – but his point is valid, and it is largely because of the accountants' domination that it is so difficult for new authors to get themselves published unless their books are immediately and obviously commercial. In fiction particularly, publishers are very reluctant to take on new writers unless they can find a paperback publisher for the book in question, and since there are comparatively few paperback houses and their lists are already at least half filled with bestselling authors, the chances are poor. Sponsorship, whether from the Arts Council and similar bodies or from commercial firms, is badly needed for the kind of book which should be published but does not necessarily command a mass-market appeal, and for the author who needs time and encouragement while he is trying to perfect his craft and before his talent comes to full flower.

It is not just books which will make money that publishers want, but authors who will do so. Every publisher who takes an author on to his list hopes that he will produce more than one book, and indeed some titles are rejected on the grounds that the publishers believe that the author is a one-book writer. *The Egg and I* was a case in point, rejected by many publishers at least partially on those grounds, and finally taken on by the late Peter Guttmann of Hammond, Hammond (a publishing company which is, alas, no longer active), who himself doubted whether Betty Macdonald would write another book. In fact she wrote several more, and very successful they were, which was a bonus for Hammond, Hammond.

It is easy enough to say that publishers want books and authors which will make money for them – not necessarily a great deal of money, but sufficient to make a contribution towards overheads and a small profit in addition – and that the more commercial your book the easier it will be to find a publisher for it, but such comments, apart from stating the obvious, are not particularly helpful to the aspiring author. Specific advice on what publishers want is hard to give, but there are some general points to be made.

In my days as an editor, I used to look for four A's:

A for Authorship
By this I did not mean just accurate spelling and punctuation, though, as I have said elsewhere, I believe that authors who do not take trouble over this side of writing are doing themselves a disservice. I was looking for a use of words which indicated mastery over them, and that included not only using them correctly, but also a sense of style, so that sentences were well phrased and the author knew when to begin new paragraphs and chapters, and had given his book a feeling of shape and construction. I was looking for an ability to communicate ideas with clarity, and an understanding of the effect the words chosen would have on the reader. And I was looking for the book to have something to say, by which I do not mean that it necessarily had to have some significant message, but that the author had an objective in writing his book, that he had indeed something to tell the reader, whether it was how to decorate the bathroom or what James I was really like, or whether it was simply a good story.

A for Authenticity
I looked for credibility of characters and plot in a novel, for a true sense of period and place, and if a problem were presented, for a genuine solution to it rather than any *deus ex machina* contrivance. If I were asked to suspend disbelief, I

was willing to do so just so long as the author remained faithful to the conventions he had originally established. I did not want anything to take me out of the story by forcing me to say, "I don't believe that". Although "A for Authenticity" belongs chiefly to fiction of all kinds, where realism or at least mock-realism is currently the fashion (started, I believe, largely by *Z-Cars*, the first semi-documentary fiction that we saw on our television screens), to some extent the same criteria can be applied to most books. You might sum it up by calling it "a sense of truth".

A for Action

In the detective novels which were popular between the two World Wars, it quite often happened that the first half dozen chapters were taken up with descriptions of the country house and the guests who were staying there, and it was only in Chapter Seven that a body appeared in the locked library. That approach is not much in favour nowadays, and readers want a body on page one, or very soon after, and the action must from that moment on be continuous and reasonably fast-paced. This criterion sounds again as though it applied only to fiction, and the special field of mysteries at that, but that is far from the case. I looked, whatever kind of book I was dealing with – the book on decorating the bathroom or the biography of James I are adequate examples – for my interest to be seized from the very beginning, and for the author never to relax the grip he had on me. This is one reason why first paragraphs are so important. So too is reader identification, a term which is usually applied to fiction, but which is relevant to any kind of book you can think of – the reader has to feel involved and interested and, though he may not recognize this consciously, that the book is written for him.

A for Authority

This really applies only to non-fiction, and refers not only to the fact that the author must have a full command of his subject, so that he can write with authority about it, but also that he should have acceptable qualifications for writing the book. I have already, in the last chapter, touched on the problem of the unknown, non-historian writer who produces a new biography of Mary, Queen of Scots – unless he has exceptional talents he will find it very difficult to force his way into a sphere dominated by biographers who are either accredited historians or well-known authors, and who frequently can claim to be in both those categories. It applies just as much to a book on gardening, or economics, or the theatre, or whatever the subject may be. Of course, it is not only a question of qualifications, but that the author's authority also depends on his name being known at least to some degree by those people who are likely to want to read the book, a factor which makes it much easier to sell.

One other quality which publishers look for, needless to say (or is it?) is originality, though it is true that there are some houses which prefer to tread well-worn paths and publish books almost indistinguishable from those that they have brought out successfully in the past and which they know exactly how to sell effectively. Even these conventional publishers, though looking for a book which is written to a proven popular formula, will be drawn to the typescript which is original in some aspect – the style, perhaps, or the humour and wit, or the twist in the plot which gives a new angle on a familiar theme. It is always difficult for authors to be original without venturing into the experimental (which is rarely likely to command a large enough market to interest the average general publisher), but if you can bring a touch of individuality to your book, it will stand a better chance of success.

A highly controversial book is almost always of interest, but not if it steps beyond the bounds of the publisher's taste, or if it is likely to run foul of the law (this kind of book is often libellous), or if it is too topical and its subject is likely to have faded from the news by the time the book could be published. Authors of controversial books do need too some authority, as defined above.

Naturally, there are exceptions to all these rules and guidelines – publishing is so individual and bizarre and multifaceted that every statement one makes about it needs qualification – and books which do not meet any of the requirements listed above, or which do so only partially, are frequently and often successfully published. It can be very confusing for authors, especially when they compare their own rejected work with books which have been published, perhaps by the very firm which rejected theirs, and decide, with as much dispassion as they can contrive, that the published books are inferior to their own work.

The first thing to remember is that you cannot compare like with unlike. If you are what is known as a serious novelist and you look at the romantic novels that are published and think how feeble and contrived and despicable they are in comparison with your own work, or if you are an academic who can see no justification for the success of certain pseudo-scientific books based on imagination rather than solid evidence, do remember that these books are not written for you, that they have their own market, their own techniques, and that the people who write them are mostly extremely capable craftsmen who know exactly what they are doing and do it with considerable flair.

"All right," you may say, "I will compare my work only with those who write in the same vein as I do. How is it that X and Y, who don't write as well as I do and whose subjects are more limited in interest than mine, get published when I can't? I can only think that they are friends of the publisher." Well, they may be, but I doubt very much whether that is the principal reason why their books were accepted for publication, or indeed whether it had any influence on the decision at all. It may simply be a matter of taste – the publisher may disagree with your assessment of X and Y's work in comparison with your own, and has published them because in his opinion their books are better than yours. Books are accepted for publication not by some impartial and infinitely wise committee of assessors, but by individuals with their own likes and dislikes. Or it could be that X and Y are on that publisher's list because they submitted their books to him at a time when he was looking for just such work and theirs were the best that came along; now that he has them on the list, he has no room for your book, though he might even prefer it to one of the others. Or maybe X and Y are already established to some degree, and even though the publisher may not feel that their latest books are up to the standard he would like, he believes in them and wants to go on publishing them, hoping that their next books will be better. As I have already suggested, publishers are interested in authors rather than in books – by which I mean that they are looking for a writer who, with a number of books, will build up a reputation so that his books sell in increasing numbers as each new one comes out, or who, if his first book is an immediate success, will repeat that success with many more books.

Of course, the bigger name you are as an author, the more you have the publisher at your mercy, not only in securing better terms for yourself, but sometimes in persuading him to publish books that you have written at which he might otherwise have looked askance. If he refuses to take the book on, he knows that with your reputation you will find no difficulty in placing it with another house, which will be only too glad to publish it, however bad it may be, in order to get you on their list. I would suggest, however, that if you are just such a world-famous author and your publisher exhibits doubts about your latest offering, you should listen to him seriously before rushing into the arms of one of his competitors. Bad books can damage even the most brilliant of reputations.

The most important point to remember in what I have already said when, as a frustrated author once said to me, "you look at some of the rubbish that does get published", is that the publication of a book still depends, despite the influence of the accountants, on the personal tastes of an editor. Editors, believe it or not, are human, and the variety of their individual quirks and foibles is infinite. I could cite dozens of cases in which colleagues of mine in various editorial departments have been tremendously enthusiastic about books in which I could see no merit at all. Sometimes they proved me wrong, sometimes my doubts were justified. All editors make mistakes, all editors have successes which astonish their colleagues; all editors turn down books which subsequently become bestsellers, all editors champion books which do well against all the odds. *Jonathan Livingstone Seagull* is a fine case in point; the book landed on the desk of an editor called Eleanor Friede, who was enthusiastic about it and more or less forced through its publication; for some years the book seemed to justify the reservations of the Jeremiahs and was counted as a failure, but it then suddenly became a "cult" book and a world bestseller.

Some authors feel very aggrieved that certain books, often with little to distinguish them from the herd, and in some cases even of below average quality, get "hyped" into bestsellerdom. How does it happen? It usually begins with the enthusiasm of an agent, who begins to talk the book up and persuades a publisher to believe that the book is a potential bestseller, worth a lot of money. One such sale usually allows the bandwaggon to roll, and the book sells for extravagant sums all over the world. There is often an element of the Emperor's New Clothes about it. It certainly isn't fair, when much better books earn their authors little or no money, but then life isn't fair, and success in any field nearly always depends on a certain amount of luck as well as ability. You have to be in the right place at the right time; you, or your agent, must recognize that right time and right place and seize the opportunity when it comes – and there is a great element of luck in that too.

Do hyped books work? Well, sometimes, but often they fall flat. When they do succeed it is usually because the book which is chosen for such an exercise has the quality of being in tune with the reading public's mood, a concept which is well explored in Claud Cockburn's examination of popular fiction, *Bestseller*. Of course, although publishers are generally agreed that advertising, other than to the trade, does not sell books, the hyped book is often very widely advertised, and that happens because, if the publisher is going to print, and presumably sell, a very large quantity of the book, he can afford to spend a large enough sum of money on advertising for it to have some effect on his sales.

Why, given two books of similar merits and accord with public taste, does one attract the hype approach while the other is neglected? Because of the irrationality of the human element, and because of the way the wheel of fortune turned. The hyped book just happened to appeal to a small handful of people who believed that it could be promoted into bestseller-dom and were prepared to spend money to push it in that direction; and it had the right kind of luck.

Since it is so difficult to be specific about what publishers want, it may be helpful to take the easier course of saying what they don't want.

Topical books
The normal publishing process takes about nine months from the acceptance of a finished typescript to publication – longer if the book is complicated in some way (e.g. an illustrated book with a complex layout). Books can be produced in a much shorter time, and sometimes are – almost instant publication takes place for an event like the death of Churchill, the raid on Entebbe, the wedding of Prince Charles and Lady Diana Spencer, but these are exceptions, mostly paperbacks, and the event is of such wide interest that a really massive sale can be envisaged, thus justifying the enormous extra effort and expense that are necessary to whittle the normal nine

months down to a few days. But a topical book without a huge market will have little appeal to any publisher, especially as so often its topicality, which will have disappeared by the time the book comes out, is its only merit.

Categories of books not normally on his list
Publishers sell to booksellers, and booksellers tend to think of publishers as specialist in certain areas. Thames & Hudson, for instance, are known as publishers of art books. Now, if a publisher who has not previously entered that field (let us call them "Rows & Crowne") brings out an art book, the bookseller's first reaction may often be, "If it were any good, Thames & Hudson (or one of the other art book publishers) would be bringing this out. Since Rows & Crowne are publishing it, it's probable that Thames & Hudson and the other specialist houses have turned it down. Therefore it can't be much good. QED. No, I won't order any copies, thank you." That is of course an over-simplification, and booksellers will deny that they can be so conservative and shortsighted as to turn down a saleable book simply because it bears an unexpected imprint, but it is certainly true that publishers find it quite difficult to broaden the scope of their lists because of trade resistance. The moral from the author's point of view is that he must do his market research thoroughly, and if his book is a specialist one, not send it to a publisher who is unlikely to want to experiment with it in a field which is unfamiliar to him.

The jack of all trades
Publishers, booksellers and the public like to know where they are with an author. They like him to write the same sort of book each time, and it is certainly much easier to build a reputation as an author if you stick to one field, however loosely. But there is another reason why publishers tend to look a little doubtfully at an author who offers them a series of widely differing books, and that is that the jack of all trades is so frequently master of none. If you can write a book on any subject under the sun, you may be quite brilliant – or possibly you deserve the rather uncomplimentary description of a hack writer. The one thing that shrinking markets have done for books is to improve their overall quality. There is far less room for the hack than there used to be.

Autobiographies

Everyone, they say, has a book in him. True, but in most cases it should stay there, principally because so few people have the ability to get it out of themselves in a form that anyone else will want to read. But one of the other problems is that the book which most people have in them and want to write is their own life story. "I have had such an interesting life. I'm sure I could write a book about it," or, "After all your experiences, you should write a book – you really should." Unfortunately, thousands upon thousands of men and women lead lives which they and their friends find of riveting interest, but unless they are famous, or infamous, or can write superbly and perhaps evocatively of a bygone age, few readers outside their immediate circle will find it equally absorbing. And if you cannot claim fame or the pen of a Laurie Lee, who is going to buy the book? Your friends and relations will expect to be given copies, or will get the book out of the library; no one else will bother. Write the book, by all means, for your children and grandchildren to read, but don't expect to get it published commercially. This advice also applies to humorous accounts of your experiences – especially about moving house, a favourite subject for amateur authors. Almost everyone's experience of moving house is traumatic and, if you have that sort of sense of humour, funny, which means that in order to write about it successfully, your experiences or your humour (and preferably both) should be exceptional, so that the book is lifted beyond the commonplace.

Biographies of obscure historical personages

You may have discovered the truth about Sir Humphrey Drivell, the dull, stay-at-home eighteenth-century squire of the village of Upton Downbottom, but unless your account of his life, like *The History of Myddle*, for instance, also gives an unusual and detailed account of an eighteenth-century village community, few people are going to want to buy or borrow the book. No one has ever heard of Sir Humphrey Drivell, and that means that very few people will want to read about him. The same applies to a history of St Ethelwulf's Church, Upton Downbottom; you may be able to find a local printer who will produce a few copies for the benefit of the Upton Downbottom villagers and you and your relatives and friends, but the market for the book will be so small that no commercial publisher is likely to be interested. Again, I would not wish to discourage anyone from writing such a book, which might be fascinating and of immense value to its very limited audience. Just don't expect to get it published.

Short stories
I have never understood, nor, I think, have most publishers, why short stories are generally so unsuccessful. Everyone you talk to swears that he adores them, yet unless you are a very well-established writer, you are most unlikely to get a volume of short stories published, and even if you are at the top of the bestselling tree, your short stories will be given a much smaller print quantity than your new novel. Short stories do still get published occasionally in anthologies, and there is a limited market for them in collections of science fiction and horror.

Poetry
There are still a few publishers in the world who are prepared to publish poetry, although it is almost certainly going to lose them money to do so. For the most part, however, the influence of the accountants has meant that publishers do not even consider taking on a volume of poetry, unless, again, the poet has an already very well-established name. Luckily there are many small specialist firms which devote themselves to poetry, often published in duplicated form, so there is still some outlet for this important kind of writing, though the financial rewards are likely to be minuscule.

Bandwaggon books
As soon as a certain style of book becomes a bestseller – *The Day of the Jackal*, for instance, or the James Bond stories – half the authors of the world seem to rush to their typewriters to produce imitations. There are two reasons why they are not often successful: the first is that few of these imitators are talented enough to write books which are anywhere near as good as the originals; the second is that such fashions in writing can often change remarkably rapidly, and by the time you have written your imitation, and allowing for the normal delay in getting a publisher to accept it and then publish it, the fashion may have disappeared.

Obscene, scurrilous or politically extreme books
This is a question of doing your market research thoroughly.
There are markets for books of this kind, but don't expect a
publisher whose list is middle-of-the-road to take on an
outrageously sexy book, or send your far-right orientated
book to a left-wing publisher. As for the scurrilous books,
beware of the laws of libel (see p. 62).

Children's books
The editors of children's books are usually people of enormous patience. Scores of mothers and grandmothers make up
stories for their little ones, decide when they are well received
by their young audience that they could be published, and
send them to a publisher, often accompanied by illustrations
done by a friend whose lack of talent is equalled only by that
of the story-teller. Writing for children is extremely difficult,
and has not been made easier by the fact that nowadays it is
essential to be non-sexist, non-racist, and the length, complexity and especially the vocabulary of the story must be
acceptable for the age range for which the book is intended. It
is really a most difficult market to break into, and it becomes
very little easier as you move up the age scale, coming
eventually to teen-age novels. All writing for young people is
difficult. If you can get it right, you will be welcomed, but be
prepared for disappointment. And if you send in illustrations,
do make sure that they are of professional standard.

Novels about failures
The plain fact is that failures are usually rather boring, simply
because they are failures. You need exceptional skills to make
them interesting.

Expensive books
In general, publishers don't want books that are very expensive to produce because they are intended to be in odd shapes
and sizes or because they involve the pasting in of pull-outs
and pop-ups and other gimmicks, or which demand to be
printed in seven colours throughout. Such books are published, of course, but you certainly stand a better chance by
sticking to ordinary, common-or-garden books which can be
produced in one of the standard formats such as the traditional Demy 8vo, Crown 4to or Large Crown 8vo (or their metric
equivalents).

Libellous books

The threat of a libel action is enough to make the strongest publisher go deathly pale. Quite apart from the fact that he may be involved in an extremely expensive court case and may have to pay very heavy damages, he will perhaps also have to withdraw and destroy all copies of the book that have been printed. And although in theory he can reclaim all his losses from the author (almost all publishing contracts carry a clause under which the author agrees to indemnify the publisher if his book contains defamatory material), in practice the author rarely has the resources with which to reimburse the publisher.

It is not the province of this book to give a complete explanation of the laws of libel, but some helpful points may be made.

First of all, it does not mean that you can only write about real people, if you do not say anything nasty about them, either directly or indirectly. Only if he can show that he or his reputation has been damaged by what you have written, that he has been exposed to hatred, ridicule or contempt, can anyone sue you for libel.

Secondly, in certain circumstances, there is a possible defence to a libel suit if you can show that you had no intention of libelling the person concerned and did so by accident. If you invent, let us say, an imaginary doctor who behaves in an unprofessional way and happen to choose for him the name of a real doctor, the real doctor may sue you for libel. There is a chance that you will be able to escape by showing that you did not know of his existence and bore no malice against him, but at the least you will have to issue an apology and pay any legal costs involved. It is much better in such cases to check that no such doctor's name is entered on the BMA register, and to take similar action when concerned with other professions.

Thirdly, a straightforward defence to any libel action is that the statements complained of are true. Before you use this defence, however, you should be sure that you can prove the truth of what you have written in every respect. In any case, you may still be involved in an expensive court action if the plaintiff decides to go ahead against you.

Fourthly, you cannot libel the dead. However, you have to beware that what you say about the dead person does not in any way damage his descendants. If you say, for instance,

"Lord X came from a family noted throughout history for lechery, duplicity and total incompetence in high office", you may be referring in your mind only to Lord X himself and his forebears, but his descendants might not be at all pleased.

The possibility of libel is fairly easy to recognize in non-fiction. If you have written unpleasant things about a living person, using his name or identifying him in some other unmistakable way, then you should not be surprised if a libel case follows. In fiction, it is not quite so plain, because authors who base their supposedly fictional characters on real-life people usually change the name concerned. This is really not sufficient; if the real-life model and his friends can still recognize him as your original, then he will still have a case for libel. If you must draw your characters from real life, then you should at least disguise them as much as you possibly can, if you are going to say defamatory things about them, changing not only their names, but also the physical appearance, age, occupation, and so on. It may also help to introduce the same original, in a more recognizable form, as one of your "goodies", so that he and his friends will recognize himself in that characterization rather than in the other one. Be careful about the functions of your characters, particularly if they hold high positions in life; if, for instance, you were to write a novel in which you showed the Chairmain of the Coal Board in a very unpleasant light, the real-life holder of that office might have a case against you even though you had changed his name, appearance and other characteristics.

The notice that appears in the front of many novels, indicating that the characters in it are imaginary and bear no resemblance to any person, living or dead, is of little use. The notice won't save you if someone believes you have libelled him.

If there is anything in your book which you consider to be of a potentially libellous nature, you should bring it to the notice of your publisher. Additionally, if you are worried and your publisher does not do this, you can submit the book to a solicitor for his opinion, though it is as well to choose one who is a specialist in the field. Your publisher will know the names of suitable firms.

Let me repeat once more that there are always exceptions to prove the rule that publishers don't want the kinds of books listed above. Perhaps the chances for them are less, but you can never be quite certain because there are still a great many publishers about who are eccentric, unpredictable, erratic in their tastes as well as in the way they conduct their business. It is, after all, a fairly crazy business, in which every product is different, and each of them is, to a greater or lesser degree, a gamble. It is also a fascinating way of life (and "way of life" is the right phrase, for few people in publishing are involved in their work only during office hours), with constantly changing interest and problems, and those who work in the industry – even the maligned accountants – do so on the whole not just because of the financial rewards – there are comparatively few really rich publishers about, precisely because it is a gambling business and it is only too easy to lose on one book all the money you have made on another – but because they like books and, surprisingly enough, authors.

It was Sir Frederick Macmillan, I believe, who first said, "Publishing would be fun if it weren't for authors." Undoubtedly he had his tongue in his cheek. Authors can be infuriating, childish, disloyal, temperamental, greedy, vain and any other pejorative adjectives that you can think of – just like other human beings. Publishers can be all those things too – just like other human beings. On the whole, publishers are eager to love and cherish their authors. They begin by loving a book, and with any luck, they will then transfer that love to its author.

That then is the message: publishers are not ogres, implacably hostile to all writers; on the contrary, they are always eager to find new books and authors on which they can lavish their affections. You don't believe it? Then send your work out and see what happens. But before you do, please remember that since fewer books are currently being published (though the annual total of new books produced in Britain is still frighteningly high), standards are rising. Be as certain as you can that your book is equipped to fight its way into a crowded market. You need to be professional, just as you would if you were entering any other field, and that includes being sure that what you write will appeal to a wide enough public.

Despite all the difficulties, I have never believed and still do not believe that there are any mute, inglorious Miltons around, unless they wish to remain mute and inglorious. Talent, like murder, will out; it may be more difficult for it to out, but if you really have it, you will get published. Just keep on trying.

4

The Publishing Process

What happens between the time that you submit a book to a publisher and its publication? Why does it take so long? Processes vary from publisher to publisher, but in general it will go something like this:

Editorial

Your typescript will arrive on the desk of an editor, or possibly on that of a secretary whose job it is to log all incoming submissions in a ledger in which what happens to the material will also be recorded. When it reaches an editor, he will probably glance briefly at it. In some cases, he will make an immediate decision as to whether he should read it himself, or pass it to an outside reader, or give it to another editor in the house who specializes in that kind of book, or reject it immediately. However, in some publishing houses, such decisions will be taken at a weekly editorial meeting.

If the book is non-fiction, and especially if its subject is specific rather than general, it will almost certainly be sent to an outside reader who is an expert in that field, and very often to more than one such authority. Apart from these specialists, many publishers also employ general outside readers, and in some firms almost all books, including fiction, are given an outside reading, either before or after the book has been considered within the house. Who are these general readers, and what are their qualifications? They are often ex-publishers, sometimes themselves authors, sometimes merely friends or acquaintances of the publisher; they are expected to know something about the market for general books, and to be able to distinguish between good and bad writing; but their main qualification is quite simply that their tastes are known to the publisher, which allows him to evaluate their comments. In any case, their function is not entirely that of giving a verdict on the books they read; they also usually provide a detailed summary of the book's contents.

If you feel anxiety that your typescript may be delivered up to the mercies of a comparatively unqualified person, then be assured that most publishers use their general outside readers primarily as "weeders" or to confirm a judgement already made in the publisher's office. If the outside reader recommends rejection, he is usually right, provided that he is reasonably experienced (and if he is not, then the book will almost certainly receive other readings before the final decision is made); if he recommends publication, then it will undoubtedly be read by other people too. While the editor's decision may be final, therefore, that of the outside reader very rarely is, and few books, other than those by established writers will be accepted on the basis of one reading only.

As I mentioned earlier, some publishers use authors on their list to read books on similar subjects. If this happens to you, you can expect to be paid for the reading and report – not a great deal, of course, but a few pounds at least. If your publisher does not pay you, then you are being exploited, and you may well consider him something of a rogue.

Although the reports on a book may be generally favourable, the editor may not yet be ready to move to the next stage, the preparation of an estimate. The readers may indicate that the book is potentially publishable, but that additional work on it is needed before it can be accepted, and in this case, the editor will perhaps invite the author to come to his offices to discuss the matter with him. Some authors approach such meetings in an aggressively defensive mood, unwilling to concede that their work is less than perfect as it stands; it is their right to do so, but it is also the publisher's right in such circumstances to decline to go ahead. More sensible authors will listen to what is said, and accept the criticisms or at least discuss the proposed alterations in a reasonable way. Good editors can contribute materially to the improvement of a book, and indeed that is their object, or should be. Bad editors sometimes want to change the whole approach of a book, and in such cases the author is fully entitled to resist, though he must be prepared to accept the fact that such resistance may result in the publisher deciding not to publish the book.

Authors whose books are rejected speedily often believe that the books have not been read at all, and some even resort to various devices to prove this (such as putting one of the pages upside down, or carefully inserting a hair between two pages of the typescript). Apart from the fact that the publisher may spot these traps and leave them unaltered, just to annoy the author, you might as well face the fact that publishers do not read every word of every typescript submitted to them. Some are rejected at a glance because they deal with subjects that the publisher does not include on his list, or perhaps because they are not of book length (authors often submit short stories to book publishers in the apparent belief that they also publish magazines, while others seem to think that ten thousand words or less will make a full-length book), but most get more attention than that.

A few pages will be read – sufficient for the editor, who usually has a considerable amount of experience and who knows what kind of books he is looking for, to decide perhaps that the book is of no interest to his firm. Or perhaps he will read more, and get some way into the book before deciding that it is too dull, or too unauthoritative, or too controversial, or simply too badly written for him to bother with. Even if he is interested, he may skip a great deal, or use a technique which I call "skim-reading", whereby one turns the pages very rapidly, letting the eye travel swiftly over the page to get a general idea of the book without reading much of it word for word; it sounds a very cavalier way to treat a submission, but editors do become expert at coping with the vast numbers of typescripts that flow into their offices day by day, and rarely fail to recognize a book which needs more serious consideration. In many houses, even these rapid rejections will be discussed at an editorial meeting, and a book may get another reading from a different editor as a result.

Publishers do make mistakes and reject books which they should have taken, but you can be assured that any typescript with a certain amount of quality and which will fit the publisher's list will be considered carefully. The publisher simply cannot afford to miss something worthwhile if he can possibly help it. Although he is in a buyer's market, the number of outstanding books that come his way is very limited, and he has no wish to let one get away. Adequate, publishable books are in better supply, but their numbers are vastly exceeded by the books which are of no interest to him, primarily because they are too badly written or do not fit his list.

Estimating

Assuming that the editorial reports are favourable and that any rewriting required is satisfactorily carried out, the book will probably be discussed again at an editorial meeting, and the go-ahead given for the preparation of an estimate. This involves consultation by the editor with the production department in order to assess the cost of manufacture, and with the sales department to gain their support for the project and to fix a tentative first print quantity and estimate of sales, so that the potential income can be calculated. Often the subsidiary rights department will also be consulted and asked to predict what subsidiary rights income may come in, and indeed in some cases the book will be shown to, for instance, paperback houses, in the hope of obtaining a firm offer for the paperback rights, the publisher's share of which will help to subsidize his hardcover edition.

Sometimes the estimate prepared will be unsatisfactory in that it does not show an adequate profit margin. In that case, the editor, or someone in one of the other departments, may suggest altering the specifications in some way – perhaps a smaller type face could be used, thus reducing the extent (i.e. the page length) of the book; perhaps a reduction in the number of illustrations could be considered; perhaps a cheaper printer could be used; perhaps the sales department could be persuaded to increase the print quantity or the retail price of the book, or both. Sometimes many estimates have to be prepared before the formula is right. When the estimate has been prepared it is then necessary in many firms to get approval from a number of department heads before the editor can finally write to the author to tell him that the firm wishes to publish his book. Often, after preparing several estimates, no satisfactory figures can be reached, and the editor then has reluctantly to reject the book.

The processes described are obviously time-consuming, which explains at least in part why authors so often have to wait so many weeks for a decision. During the waiting period it is often true that no news is good news, but equally a long delay, while it probably means that serious consideration is being given to the book, is no guarantee of ultimate acceptance.

Contract

If all has gone well, the publisher makes the author an offer to publish his book, usually specifying the advance that he is willing to pay and the basic royalties, but rarely going into other details, which await the preparation of a contract.

This will probably entail further discussions within the publishing house, so that whoever prepares the contract will get all the details right (though if the book is agented, the agent usually draws up the agreement on his own standard form). Authors should read each contract that they are sent with care. It is not a good idea, when you get your new contract from Messrs Rows & Crowne, to think that since you have already signed a number of agreements with them for previous books you can sign this one without reading it. They may have changed their basic contract form, or there may be a number of differences in the filling in of the blank spaces. If there is anything in the contract that you wish to query or change, write to the publisher about it – do not simply make alterations on the contract and return it to him, but settle any disputed points first. The Society of Authors and the Writers' Guild both offer their members detailed advice on contracts, so it may be worth your while to join, if not already a member. See also Chapter 5.

Some publishers send the author two copies of the contract – one for him to sign and return and the other, already signed by the publisher, for him to keep. If there are any changes, mark them and initial them on both copies. Other publishers send one copy of the contract only, giving the author his counterpart only after he has signed and returned the first copy. In such cases it may be a sensible precaution to take a photostat of the copy sent to you to sign before you return it; otherwise you may not be absolutely certain that the counterpart you eventually receive is exactly the same – not that your publisher is likely to cheat in this way, for most of them are honourable, but it is a cheap and easy way of protecting yourself against the few unscrupulous publishers that do unfortunately exist.

When you return your signed contract, it will be filed by the publisher, and probably consulted thereafter quite frequently – whenever any subsidiary rights are sold, when it is time for royalty statements to be prepared, and so on. In some firms an extract of the contract is made, with all relevant details on it, so that the whole document does not have to be consulted every time.

In most cases, an advance or part thereof, is payable on signature of the contract by both parties, and a note will be passed to the accounts department so that an appropriate cheque can be drawn.

Copy Editing

Once you have accepted the initial offer, the book may be passed to a copy editor, though nowadays, in an effort to cut costs, some publishers are dispensing with this stage, relying on the author himself to have done a large part of the copy editor's work, and leaving the rest of it to the production department and/or the designer, or even to the printer. What does the copy editor do? Many people think that he merely corrects the author's spelling and punctuation, but his responsibilities go far beyond that: he often checks the author's facts, he removes (or at least queries with the author) inconsistencies, he may rewrite phrases, sentences or even large parts of the book (there are many published books which should really bear the copy editor's name on the title-page as co-author), and he marks the typescript for the printer so that the latter has clear indications of, for example, italicization, indentation of paragraphs or of certain sections of the text, etc. Some authors resent the work of the copy editor, and with cause if they are unlucky enough to find one who interferes unwarrantably with the author's style or makes other totally unnecessary changes; but a first-class copy editor, who respects the author's intentions and knows his job, can make invaluable improvements. The good copy editor will in any case always consult the author concerning the changes he proposes, and a sensible author will listen co-operatively to what he has to say. Alterations should not in any case be made without the author's approval. But also see p. 145.

Production

By this time, the author will probably have been asked to supply a second copy of the typescript, if he has not already done so, and this will have been sent to the Production Department, whose designer will decide the type in which the book is to be printed, the type area on the page, the way that chapters are to begin, and other such details. If the book is extensively illustrated, the designer has a much more exacting job, since he will need to work out the sizes and shapes of illustrations and their position, and the exact amount of text which is to appear on each page. Given the designer's instructions, the production department will send the typescript to one or more printers in order to get firm estimates for the manufacture. The production department will also decide on the method of printing the book and the binding process which is to be used, and will in due course order, or allocate from existing stocks, a suitable quantity of paper for the agreed print quantity for the text and the jacket, and cloth (usually imitation cloth nowadays) for the binding.

When the final copy-edited typescript is ready, the production department will send it to the printer for composition, together with the illustrations (unless the book is to be printed by letterpress, in which case the line drawings will be sent to a blockmaker). The jacket design, together with the wording which is to appear on it, will also be sent for preparation and proofing. The brasses with which the title and author's name and publisher's imprint are stamped on the binding will also be ordered.

In due course, proofs of the book will arrive from the printer. Two sets are usually sent to the author – one for him to correct and return, the other for him to keep. The British Master Printers Federation provides a very helpful and inexpensive book on proof correcting, which can usually be obtained through your publisher. Corrections are extremely expensive – out of all proportion to the initial setting charge – and should therefore be kept to a minimum. Mistakes made by the printer are his responsibility and are not charged for, and should be corrected in a different colour ink from that used for any alterations the author wants to make. The latter, if they exceed a certain percentage of the total setting costs, will almost certainly be charged by the publisher to the author, so the rule must be to get your typescript as perfect as possible before it is sent to the printer, and to make only those changes which are absolutely essential at proof stage. Also be sure to note all corrections in the set of proofs you keep.

Proofs sometimes come in galley form, that is to say on long sheets of paper, and not divided up into the pages which will finally appear in the book. This method of proofing is used if large numbers of alterations are expected (and have been allowed for in the costing of the book!) or if the layout of the book is particularly complex. Sometimes proofs come on what looks like a computer print-out. More often page proofs are supplied, which look very much as the final book will appear, except that they have a paper cover and are probably not printed on the same kind of paper as will be used for the finished version.

Normally the publisher allows the author two to three weeks for the correction and return of proofs. While he is reading them, they may also be read by someone in the publishing house – usually the copy editor, but sometimes someone in the production department. When the author's corrected proofs come in, his alterations and those of the publisher's proof reader will be incorporated in the marked set which will be returned to the printer.

When all proofs have been corrected and returned to the printer, and when a final decision on the print quantity has been taken, the production department will pass the relevant order to the printers and binders for the manufacture of the book, and will monitor its progress through all stages up to delivery to the warehouse.

Jackets

The jacket design is usually fairly widely discussed within the publishing house. Many publishers employ an art director, whose sole responsibility is jackets. He will probably discuss the design for each book on the list with the editor concerned and with the sales department. If it is decided to produce a jacket which is purely typographical or is based on a photograph or perhaps an existing painting (e.g. a contemporary portrait of the subject of a biography), he may design and produce the jacket within the house. In such cases, the art director may not see a word of the book itself, and it is not necessary for him to do so. If, on the other hand, the jacket is to carry a specially commissioned illustration, he is likely to read the book so that he can brief an outside artist, who will often be given a copy of the typescript or a proof so that he too can read it. The artist will then usually submit a "rough" – a sketch of what is proposed as the final art work. This will be considered and approved or rejected by the editorial and sales departments. Increasingly the author is consulted about jackets, and many publishers welcome comments, provided that the author does not make unreasonable demands. An author's complaint about the factual accuracy of the jacket design is entirely valid, but adverse comments on the overall effect or the basic design, though he should certainly make any such criticisms and the publisher should take note of them, are less likely to be matters on which he can put his foot down. In general, publishers take a great deal of care with jackets, knowing that they are a vital sales tool, and if the sales department in particular is satisfied with the general design, the author may have to bow to their belief that it is acceptable. Not unnaturally, publishers tend to believe in their own expertise, and may well tell you bluntly that your skill is in writing the book, and theirs in knowing how best to sell it.

Subsidiary Rights

The work of the subsidiary rights department often begins at an early stage. Extra copies of the typescript may be made, but in other cases proofs will be supplied, so that the book can be submitted to paperback publishers, bookclubs, magazines and newspapers, and to foreign publishers. Some of these submissions may be delayed until finished copies of the book are available, but it is usually important to sell subsidiary rights, whenever possible, in advance of publication, especially where bookclubs are concerned, since the quantity taken by the bookclub may affect the publisher's print order.

The efforts of the subsidiary rights department are ongoing. Sometimes simultaneous submissions will be made (to all the leading paperback publishers, for example), but often it is a matter of trying one possible purchaser after another. Subsidiary rights managers are usually tenacious, and will often continue to try to sell their rights long after publication, and sometimes with considerable success. Of course, if your book is of a highly specialized nature, there may be a very limited number of potential outlets for it, and once they have all been tried, the subsidiary rights manager will understandably abandon the effort, to reactivate it only if some new buyer comes upon the scene.

The subsidiary rights department conducts the initial negotiations for the sale of rights, and in some firms is responsible for all details of the agreements, while in others the final arrangements will be made by the contracts department.

Sales

The sales department often plays a crucial part in the shaping of a publisher's list, not only in the decisions whether to accept this or that book, but also in reporting trends, sometimes suggesting specific titles or areas of publishing to the editors, and of course in the forecasting and budgeting processes which most businesses find essential if they are to fulfil Stanley Unwin's dictum, "The publisher's first duty to his authors is to remain solvent." That is a basic truth, incidentally, which it is worth thinking about.

In well-run publishing houses there is great rapport between the editorial and sales departments, each respecting the other. Unfortunately, all too often there is instead antagonism. "The sales department makes no effort with all the fine books I give them," says the editor; and the sales people reply, "If only the editors would find us some good books, we could improve our figures out of all recognition." Authors may feel that there is more justice in the editor's complaint than that of the sales force; nevertheless, it is very rarely true that the sales department makes no effort. In most cases, the sales representatives, though they may have basic salaries, are also paid a commission on the sales they achieve, so they have a personal incentive in addition to the need to keep the firm in successful business and so retain their jobs.

The larger publishing houses have their own sales forces, a team which works exclusively for that house, but smaller publishers may group together to share a sales force, or use freelance representatives.

As soon as a new book is given a tentative publication date, or sometimes even when it is first signed up, the sales department informs the sales force, giving as many details about the book as possible at that stage, and selling then begins. However, the main vehicle of communication between the publishing house and its sales force in respect of new books is the Sales Conference, at which someone, often the editors concerned, will tell the salesmen about the books, endeavouring to enthuse them and trying to give them all the information which will help them to sell the book. Although many editors have never themselves been "on the road", especially nowadays when it is no longer the habit for new entrants to the publishing business to spend some time in every department, they all need to be salesmen too, for they have to "sell" their new books in the first place to the Sales Director before it is even signed up, and then to the representatives at the sales conference. If they fail to convince the salesmen of the value of the books, then, although they will still try hard, they will obviously not approach booksellers and other purchasers with the same confidence.

Sometimes authors are invited to attend the sales conference. If this should happen to you, remember that you have two things to do: you have to convince the sales force of the quality and sales potential of your book, emphasizing any special markets which would be particularly interested in it; and you have to persuade them, if you can, that you are a likeable person, since it is after all a part of human nature to try a little harder for a friendly, pleasant author than for one who is perhaps too conceited or stand-offish or who talks down to the reps. If you are invited to speak at a sales conference and the whole idea terrifies you because, like many authors, you are extremely shy or because you know that you are an abysmal speaker, then it is probably best to decline and leave the job of presenting your book to the editor. Don't be surprised or hurt if you are not asked to attend a sales conference – it is a rare honour.

Of course it is not only to booksellers that the publisher sells his books. Wholesalers, library suppliers and, of particular importance to the British trade which depends so much on its ability to export, the overseas outlets all have to be canvassed. The publisher's regular customers are called on at regular and fairly frequent intervals, but for some of the smaller shops the period between calls may be a long one, so it is important that the representatives should have all the necessary information about new books well in advance, so that they can be sure that everyone on whom they call will have heard of the book and had the opportunity to order – or rather, to be persuaded to do so. It is important to remember that there is no obligation on any bookseller to order any given book. He has to be persuaded by the publisher's rep that he should do so.

How the salesman does this is with personal enthusiasm, by using his knowledge of the customer (in some cases he may indeed "make no effort", knowing that the bookseller concerned has no market for that particular book), by trading on his own reputation (if he has guided the bookseller wisely in the past, his advice will be more readily taken) and that of his firm (which includes not only the quality of its list, but also its record in such matters as prompt delivery and its vigour in publicity and promotion). Of course, he uses jackets, catalogues and advance information sheets, which are the most common sales aids. Sometimes the bookseller will be given a proof copy of the book, so that he can form his own judgement. Not all the sales that the rep makes are "firm" – many are "on sale or return", meaning that the bookseller has the facility of returning the books to the publisher for credit if, after a reasonable period, he has failed to sell any or all of them. Very often it is only by such methods that the rep can persuade the bookseller to order the book, and when you consider how many books are published every year, it is hardly surprising that he often fails.

Many of the chains of bookshops have central buying arrangements, and often it is the Sales Director himself who deals with these large accounts, and calls on them and sells the list.

The sales department is also primarily responsible for calling for reprints, which, incidentally, is always a matter for great care, for though all copies of the publisher's edition may have left his warehouse, the sales people have to be sure that they are also leaving the booksellers' shelves and that sufficient re-orders are likely to come to justify the reprint. The sales department also arranges special deals such as sponsored books (though the editors may take a major part in this), National Book Sales, and the kind of offer which involves saving the tops of cereal packets and sending them off in order to buy a book at a reduced price.

And then they sell "remainders". Remainders are those copies of a book which are left when sales have come down to an extremely low level or have ceased altogether. At that point, the sales department will probably decide that the book should be remaindered, and will approach a remainder merchant. The latter is a kind of specialist wholesaler, who purchases unwanted books from publishers at a very low figure indeed (usually less than the cost of manufacture), and then sells them, mostly through specialized outlets, to the public at knock-down prices. See also p. 160

Publicity and Promotion

Publicity and promotion are vital tools of the sales department, and in many firms the department is under the direct control of the Sales Director.

Since this is the area in which many authors feel that their publishers fail most dismally, I shall examine it in some detail.

When your book is accepted for publication, you will probably be asked to fill in a form asking for such information as any bookshops where you are personally known, any papers or journals where your book has an especially good chance of being reviewed, any organizations which might be circulated with details of your book. Authors should fill these forms in with care, despite the fact that some publishers seem thereafter to file the forms away and to take no action on any of the author's suggestions. Good publishers do follow the information through, though sometimes they may neglect certain aspects, usually because of a lack of sufficient money in the publicity budget.

When hard times come (and they never appear to be totally absent as far as publishers are concerned), the publicity and promotion budget is almost always the first place where the publisher looks for economies, and the people who work in that department are used to doing so on a shoestring. The amount of money that they are allocated in any given year has to be spread among all the books that the firm is publishing in that period, and not surprisingly, when you stop to think about it, the books on which most money is spent are likely to be those which the publisher considers the major ones on his list, and this means that once they have been allocated their large share of the budget, the lesser books split the remainder between them, and end up with very little each. Hence, perhaps, your publisher's inability to produce the leaflet you envisaged, and hence almost certainly his reluctance to advertise your book in the National Press.

In fact, publishers believe, almost to a man, that National Press advertising is a waste of money. In the modern jargon, it is cosmetic, serving only to appease the author and satisfy his ego. "But if the book is not advertised," you may say, "how will the public know about it?" Well, there are other ways, which we will come to in a moment, but be honest – do you really buy books because you have seen them advertised in the National Press? All right, you do – but you are an exception. The vast majority of people buy books (or more often borrow them) because they have read a review, or because of recommendation by word-of-mouth or from a bookseller, or simply because they happen to see it (paperbacks in particular are known to be "impulse buys"). Publishers are slightly less grudging towards local newspapers, which are much cheaper and possibly of some value if the author is known in the area where they circulate, but even then usually feel that their money can be better spent elsewhere. One of the truths of the advertising business is that a small amount of money is not nearly as cost-effective as a large amount, and alongside that principle it can also be said that something which is not already in demand can only be stimulated effectively by a blanket coverage. Indeed, two or three hundred pounds spent on advertising in the National Press is likely to achieve nothing, whereas two or three thousand pounds may begin to bring results. If you don't believe me, ask any advertising agent.

Publishers prefer to concentrate on the trade, for it is to the trade that they sell their wares, not to the general public, and the battle for the success of a book is a long way towards being won if they can persuade the bookshops and the wholesalers to order good quantities.

The first thing that they do is to produce a catalogue of their new titles. Your book will appear in the catalogue, sometimes accompanied by an illustration – perhaps your photograph, or a reproduction of the jacket, or an illustration from the book – but almost invariably with a blurb. The blurb is of course the description of the book which normally appears on the front flap of the jacket and very often on the first page of the book too. Your publisher may indeed ask you to supply a blurb for your book, though he will usually discard your effort or rewrite it substantially, because the majority of authors do not excel at describing their own books succinctly and appealingly, and however big their egos often shrink from using the adulatory adjectives beloved of professional blurb-writers. You have a moral right (and a legal one too, if you have signed an agreement such as the one discussed in Chapter 5) to see and approve your blurb, but your criticisms will be best confined to matters of fact.

The blurb, or perhaps a shortened version of it, will appear then in the catalogue, as will a tentative publication date and price and various other details about the book, many of which pieces of information will turn out to be inaccurate, because catalogues are prepared a long time in advance of the publication of most of the books in them, and changes in plan frequently occur. Your position in the catalogue may give you cause for thought. How exciting to find your book occupying the leading position! How humiliating to find that your masterpiece is tucked away at the back and has been given no more than a quarter page! In the latter case, you may feel hard done by, but you just have to accept the fact that although most publishers believe all their geese to be swans until publication proves otherwise, they do recognize that some are swannier and some geesier than others. If your publisher sees your book as belonging in the geesier section of his catalogue, it's hard luck.

The catalogue is sent out to the trade (booksellers, purchasers of subsidiary and foreign rights, etc.) and some copies go to members of the public who have asked to be placed on the firm's mailing list. Sometimes the catalogue is used as an insert in the Export edition of *The Bookseller*, which is the major trade paper (well worth subscribing to) and which twice a year produces huge Export numbers in which almost all publishers present their lists of new books for the coming months. The Export number is a kind of gigantic multi-publisher catalogue. It also contains extensive and informative editorial coverage of forthcoming books.

The publisher may also insert other advertisements for your book in *The Bookseller* and other trade papers. These will appear in advance of publication, but not usually as early as the Export numbers. He may also be willing to place advertisements in specialist journals catering for the section of the public for whom the book is intended.

Leaflets are sometimes prepared and sent out, but usually only for specialist books in which the recipients of the leaflet are likely to be keenly interested. The publisher needs to be sure of a good return from such publicity, for the cost of printing leaflets, plus envelopes and the labour of addressing them, and above all postage, is often prohibitive.

Sometimes a publisher will send proof copies of a book to well-known people, in the hope of getting pre-publication "puffs" from them, which might be quoted on the leaflet, if there is one, or on the jacket, or in advertisements. A proof copy may also go to those journalists who write about forthcoming books in the trade Press. Of course, they cannot mention every new book, so there is no guarantee that yours will be covered.

The publisher may also prepare showcards and other material for use in bookshops. This is known as "point of sale" material. Usually it is reserved for major titles, but if your local bookshop is willing to put on a display of your new book, your publisher may be willing to supply a special showcard proclaiming the fact that you are a local author.

One of the most important weapons in the publicity department's armoury is the review copy. Most publishers send out large numbers of review copies – sometimes as many as two hundred – to the literary editors of all major national and provincial newspapers and magazines, to specialist publications, to radio and television programmes, and indeed to any person or organization which might review the book. Many authors are bitterly disappointed by the lack of reviews for their books, and often blame the publisher. But it is not really his fault, and he is often as disappointed as you are. Reviews are important – even a bad one, unless it is totally destructive, is said to be better than none – and if you have any influence with a reviewer it is worth making sure that he gets a copy of your book.

A regular feature of publishing life is the parties that publishers throw to launch certain of their books. Some authors find it very disheartening when their publishers tell them that they have no intention of celebrating publication in that way, and even decline an offer from the author to share the expense. Why should they refuse? Well, again it's a matter of cost-effectiveness. The guests at such a party are made up generally of the author and a few of his family and close friends, a fair sprinkling of the publisher's staff, a few journalists and literary editors, and a bookseller or two. Large amounts of liquor are consumed. The object of the exercise is to get publicity for the book and to persuade the booksellers to order it, but the amount of space that the Press gives on these occasions is usually very limited, and the booksellers present have already ordered the book if they are going to do so. So little is achieved. If your publisher does throw a party for you, you can consider yourself honoured indeed.

The publicity and promotion department also spends quite a lot of its time trying to get the firm's authors radio and television interviews, speaking engagements at literary luncheons, and the like. In the United States, where every city of any size has its own TV station, and television broadcasting is almost round-the-clock, a great deal of air time is taken up with "chat shows", which makes it comparatively easy to get authors the chance to talk about their books on TV. In this country, with our limited number of programmes, it is far more difficult, and the average author's chances of getting on a book programme or nationally-screened interview shows are very small. The recent opening up of many local radio stations has improved matters in that direction, and you may well have the chance of a local broadcast. Luncheons and other speaking engagements are fairly rare, and depend in any case partly on your ability to speak well. If you can work up a good talk it may prove worthwhile publicity for you and your book, and you may be asked to give it to Writers' Circles and local Literary Societies, and Women's Institutes and Townswomen's Guilds, and so on. You will also in most cases receive fees for your talks, or at least expenses, which are sometimes offered in an amount which will exceed your actual costs and therefore amount to expenses plus a small fee. It is impossible to give guidance on the fees that one might expect. The Society of Authors suggested in the Winter 1981 issue of *The Author* a minimum of £40 plus expenses, but this is quite unrealistic for the average WI, for example which would probably not expect to pay more than £10. Get as big a fee as you can, and if it is not very much, console yourself with the thought that the publicity is worth having.

The publicity and promotion department will also be involved, along with the sales department, in film tie-ins and other similar marketing opportunities, and arranges tours for some authors, though again these are usually reserved for the more famous. Tours are exhausting – a series of frantic train and car journeys, interspersed with drink parties and a great deal of hand-shaking with local booksellers, journalists and other worthies. They also usually involve signing sessions. Most publishers and most booksellers hate signing sessions. They are surprisingly costly to arrange, so that only the most successful of them are profitable. And how many are really successful? Very, very few – usually only when the author is a nationally known "personality". Far more often it is an extremely depressing occasion, with the bookshop manager, the publisher's publicity manager and his local representative making embarrassed conversation while the author sits miserably behind a pile of his books, waiting for the customers who don't come. And if one does come, it is quite likely to be the representative's wife, summoned by a desperate phone-call. Do everyone a favour, including yourself, and don't ask your publisher to arrange a signing session for you.

In some ways you yourself can do as much for the book as anyone else, and you should not be shy about blowing your own trumpet. Unless your book is too technical for them, your relations and friends will read it. Don't hesitate to ask them to recommend it in turn to their friends and to give copies of it for Christmas and birthday presents. Most non-writers find authors curiously glamorous, and you should not hesitate to capitalize on this. Tell a stranger that you are an author, and he will almost always show immediate interest and ask what sort of books you write. Don't be modest, but do your best to make him resolve to go and buy a copy. If your book is going to be paperbacked, keep quiet about it for as long as you can, so that people buy the hardcover edition instead of waiting for the cheaper version. Use every trick you can think of to increase your sales.

By the way, that includes not being too generous with your complimentary copies. You will probably be forced to give free copies to your nearest and dearest, but make the others buy their own. You can promise that when they've done so you will sign the copy for them.

Final Print Quantity, Price and Publication Date

After the proofs have been returned, a final decision about the print quantity will be taken. This may vary from the figure originally discussed for the purposes of the estimate when the book was first under consideration. Very often, alas, the print quantity is lowered. Why? Because publishers, who are among the world's optimists, become less so as the time approaches for them to commit themselves to spending large sums of money on the gamble of manufacturing a book. Additionally, it is often difficult to maintain the initial enthusiasm – new books have come along to engage the editor's attention, and he may be far more interested in the one that he is about to sign up than in the one on which, although it is not yet published, his work was completed months ago. That does not mean that he has lost his enthusiasm totally – it is a matter of degree. Sales departments like to be cautious, and the editor may not fight them as vigorously now as he would have done earlier to keep the print quantity up or even increase it. Other circumstances may affect the decision too. For instance, the failure to sell subsidiary rights may have lessened confidence in the book, or the market may have changed in some respect, or the book have been pre-empted by another publisher's book on the same subject, or advance orders may, for these reasons or for no discernible cause, have been disappointing. Equally of course there may have been reasons why the print quantity should be increased – bolstered by success in the subsidiary rights market and initial reactions from booksellers, excitement about the book may have mounted. Or it may be that the publisher is going to stick with the number he first thought of. Whatever print quantity is decided upon, new sets of figures will probably be prepared, now that the costs of the book are more accurately known, and again approval for the estimate will have to be obtained from various departments within the publishing house.

The book's price will also be fixed. This is not an easy matter. The public at large believes that books are expensive, though in fact they are remarkably cheap when you compare them with the ephemeral delights of eating out, or going to the cinema or theatre, or indeed if you compare them with almost any other consumer item. Be that as it may, the publisher needs to price his books so that the return to him covers his manufacturing costs, the author's royalty, his overheads, and gives him a profit, since he is in business, after all, to make money. If he prices the book too cheaply, he will lose on it; if it is too expensive, he may find it unsaleable. The more copies he prints, the easier the decision is, for the fixed costs on the book (i.e. the composition or setting of the book in type, the preparation of the illustrations, the setting up of the printing and binding machines, the cost of originating the jacket, including the artist's fee, and other similar items) are spread over the entire printing, which means that the total costs per copy diminish the more copies are printed. With a small print quantity, however, he often finds himself in great difficulty, especially if the book is fiction, for there is a convention within the trade and among the public that fiction should cost less than a non-fiction book of similar length and size. The novel that is currently priced at £6.95 would probably cost £8.95 or more if it were, say, a biography, even without illustrations.

The cost of a book in relation to its retail price varies from publisher to publisher and from book to book, but very roughly it could be said that the average discount to wholesalers and retailers is about 40% (this allows for the higher discounts given to overseas customers), manufacturing costs work out at about 20% and the author's royalty at 10%, leaving 30% to cover the publisher's overheads (including wages, telephone and mailing costs, rent, rates, interest on capital, advertising and promotion, distribution, heating and lighting, depreciation, and the cost of the books that he does not sell, either because they are given away for promotional purposes or because he has printed too many copies) and profit, not to mention tax. The formula works out slightly differently for paperbacks, the average discount being 48%, manufacture 17.5% and the author's royalty 7.5%, leaving 27% for the publisher's other expenses and his profit, the net amount of which may not exceed 3%. It is not a formula for instant wealth for publishers, any more than it is for authors, and indeed it is worth remembering that publishing is in fact a small and not over-lucrative business. The turnover of the entire British publishing industry does not approach that of a single firm such as ICI, and even at the highest level those who work in the business rarely earn high salaries and certainly do not have the same sort of regular inflow of wealth that some of their bestselling authors enjoy. Bear in mind also that the publisher's profit is more often than not ploughed back into the firm for use on future projects, many of which will not come to fruition for many years, and the next time your affluent publisher takes you to an expensive lunch, just think how many books have to be sold to pay for it.

At the same time as the print quantity and price are decided, the publication date will probably be firmly fixed. Publishers tend to bring out their books on dates which are regular to the firm concerned – the last Thursday in the month, for instance, or the first and third Tuesdays – and usually publish more than one book on those days, so that the titles can be invoiced and despatched at the same time. The decision about which month in which to bring out a particular book depends on a number of issues. First of all, there is the question of when the manufacturing processes will have been completed and stocks delivered to the publisher's warehouse, and this in turn depends on everything going through as planned, without an unexpected delay at proof stage, for instance, or a sudden essential change of jacket design, and with the manufacturers keeping to the scheduled dates and producing work of acceptable quality; secondly, it will depend on the balance of the publisher's list – he will not want to publish all his major titles in the same month, nor, if he is a general publisher, to have nothing but fiction one month and nothing but non-fiction the next; thirdly, he will be concerned about the time of year and sometimes with specific dates – it is no use hoping to catch the important Christmas market by publishing in November or December, by which time the booksellers will have ordered all that they want for the gift season, nor is there much to be gained by publishing a book about Wimbledon, as an example, in August when the Tennis Championships are over. Incidentally, it is worth pointing out that the Christmas market is important for a limited number of books only. Some books for children, including annuals, certain practical books, annuals for adults, and those books which would in any case be bestsellers may have substantial Christmas sales, but the vast majority of books sell no better then than at any other time, and often less well.

Sometimes authors feel that their books have been hampered by being published at the wrong time of the year. There is little that can be done about this, since it is entirely the publisher's province to decide when a book will appear. Nevertheless, most publishers being business men, they try as often as circumstances will allow to publish at the most suitable time for each book on their lists, because it is in their own interest, as well as the author's, to do so. At the same time, you have to understand that not every book can be published in September or October (which many consider to be the best possible months), since the list has to be spread throughout the year. If you ask your publisher, he will probably be able to tell you good reasons in favour of every month of the year – e.g. "January is a splendid time to be published – far fewer books come out then, so you stand a better chance, to say nothing of all those people wanting to spend their book tokens – besides which, the shops have been cleared of Christmas cards and all the other space-consuming seasonal material." Equally, when he decides to delay the book until February, he will be able to tell you that "January is a rotten month anyway – all the booksellers are stock-taking, and don't want to order any new books, especially if they've got Christmas overstocks to get rid of – whereas by

February they're looking for important new books like yours to give their New Year sales an impetus."

Invoicing, Warehousing and Despatch

Once the salesmen start selling the book, orders begin to flow into the publisher's office, where they are stored until the time comes for the preparation of invoices. Almost certainly other books will be published on the same day as yours, and the orders will be collated so that the books due for publication can all be invoiced, packed and despatched together. Books ordered before publication are "subscribed" and the total of such orders is "the subscription".

The preparation of invoices used always to be done by hand, but in many large firms nowadays a computer is used. The computer is also programmed to recognize "stopped accounts" (those which the publisher will no longer supply – perhaps because they do not pay their bills) and other outlets with which, for one good reason or another, the publisher does not wish to do business, and it will also know the discounts applicable to each outlet.

Meanwhile, the books have been delivered to the warehouse from the printer and/or binder, on a date previously arranged with the warehouse manager, who must make sure that he has space to keep them near the packing benches. Later, the books will be stored on racks, ready for repeat orders. Bulk supplies of slow-moving titles will probably be kept on the top racks, from which a fork-lift truck will be needed to remove them. They may well stay there until the book is remaindered.

The books are "looked out" according to the orders, and packed, and then distributed so that, whether they go by post, rail or road, they will arrive in the bookshops in time for publication, but not too much before, since the booksellers do not want to have their stockrooms full of books which they cannot put on sale. It is important, of course, that the book should not be on sale earlier in one outlet than another, especially if the shops are rivals in the same town, so publishers try hard not only to see that booksellers stick to the publication date, but that they themselves give the shops no excuse for not doing so. It is a tricky and complex job to get all the books out for the right date, especially as the warehouse will simultaneously be packing and despatching other, non-publication, orders, dealing with returns, answering queries, and keeping in regular touch with head office (most publishers' warehouses nowadays are separate from the administrative offices).

Publication Day

It is perhaps not surprising, with all these processes to go through, that the publication of a book is a lengthy process, usually taking at least nine months, and often longer. Bear in mind too that the various departments of your publishing house are dealing not just with your book but, at their various stages, with all the other books that they will be publishing during the next nine months, and often far ahead of that. And they will have their other problems too, of general administration, staff changes, office accommodation and the like.

When publication day comes at last, you might expect, as I did when I first entered publishing as a boy of eighteen, that the place would be humming. I envisaged presses thumping away in the basement, green-eye-shielded editors frantically answering three telephones at once and passing scribbled messages to a stream of messengers scurrying in and out. The images came, I suppose, from newspaper offices as depicted by Hollywood. In fact, publication day in a publisher's offices is like any other day – if anything, quieter. All the work on the books coming out that day has been done, and the books themselves are in the shops waiting for customers. Occasionally, with a roaring bestseller, the publisher's phone may start to ring with repeat orders, but even that is more likely to occur several days after publication, when the bookseller is certain that his stocks are reducing rapidly and that there is sufficient continuing demand to justify the re-order. If you are lucky, your editor may remember to write to you to congratulate you on publication, or may even take you out for a celebratory lunch, but don't expect it as a matter of course. If he is taking anyone out to lunch to celebrate it is likely to be the author of the most important book to be published that day, but in any case he may have forgotten, in the pressure of work on books still far away from publication, that it is indeed publication day.

After Publication

What happens to your book after publication? Probably very little, unless it has a considerable success and reprints are required. The representatives will continue to try to sell your book, but it will now be part of the backlist, and though for the first few weeks after publication they will be asking their customers for repeat orders, unless these come in regularly, the book will receive a diminishing amount of attention. This is sad, but inevitable – they have to devote the bulk of their energies to the new books which are coming out.

For a while at least, the publicity and promotion people will continue to be active, but unless something happens to revive public interest in you or the subject of your book, they will ultimately give up – there is nothing more moribund, if not dead, than the majority of last year's books, unless of course you are in the happy position of having written a best-seller or a standard work, or of being a very well-known author.

The subsidiary rights department will go on beavering away for a long time, and is often surprisingly successful with books that have otherwise been forgotten by everyone except the author.

If you are fortunate, your editor or someone else in the publishing house may give you some information from time to time about how your book is going, but in many cases authors have to wait until the royalty statement appears to know the best or the worst. You are not being kept in the dark deliberately, though it may seem so; it is largely a question of out of sight, out of mind – your editor finds it takes all his time to deal with the new books going through, and tends to forget all about you, or to think to himself, "I really must write to So-and-so," but never actually does so. It may also be, especially in some of the larger houses, that he really has little idea of how sales are going, since, absurd though it may sound, some sales departments tend to keep their information to themselves, only passing it on to the editorial department if it is either unusually good or completely disastrous. It is very frustrating for the author not to know how his book is doing, but if you ring up daily or even weekly after publication, you will probably be regarded as a considerable nuisance; on the other hand, if your publisher volunteers no information, you can reasonably ask occasionally and be justified in expecting a rather more detailed reply than, "Oh, it's doing quite well – I think."

The royalty statement, when it does arrive, may be rather less comprehensive than you might hope. The royalty arrangements on nearly every book are different, and many publishers use a kind of shorthand on their statements which makes them hard to understand. It is because they are so complicated, of course, that it takes a long time to prepare them. Normally they should be sent out within three months of the ending of the period on which they report, and those three months are a time of hectic work for the royalty department. After the statements have been sent out, the department is naturally less busy, and then is a good time, if you find the statement baffling, or if you think the figures are wrong (and it pays to check them carefully, because mistakes do occur), to go to see the Royalties Manager and ask for his help. He will probably be pleased to see you, since he comparatively rarely meets the authors whose names and sales are so familiar to him, and the poor chap often thinks of authors as glamorous persons (which you and I know not to be true!).

By this time, you will perhaps be well on the way with your next book, and the whole process will begin again. If you are a beginner, this second venture should be in some respects easier, since you know what to expect – but be prepared for variations on the theme. One of the great pleasures of a publisher's life is that his work is rarely of a totally routine nature, but changes with almost every book. The differences between one book and another can mean pleasure or disappointment for the author, so be prepared.

5

Contracts

"Barabbas was a publisher," said the poet Thomas Campbell, who was also the perpetrator of a toast to Napoleon, which horrified his fellow guests at a dinner for authors until he went on to explain, "I agree with you that Napoleon is a tyrant, a monster, the sworn foe of our nation. But, gentlemen, he once shot a publisher!" Many, many authors would agree with Campbell that publishers are thieves, or if not thieves, at least totally unscrupulous in the way that they exploit authors. Publishers naturally reply that any such statement is grossly libellous of a profession which has high risks and low profit margins, and whose honest businessmen would not retain authors on their lists if they were as wicked as that. They would admit that there are some rogues among their ranks, just as there are in any profession in the world, but they would claim that such publishers tend not to survive for long, since authors, and particularly agents, soon find them out. As for exploiting authors, they might point out that it is always easy to level that accusation at those who are in a buyer's market. There may be comparatively few wildly successful books to be found, but there is never any shortage of works which some publisher somewhere will consider publishable; if you, as the seller, do not like the terms which they, as the buyer, propose, they will probably be able to find another author of a similar book who will happily sign on the dotted line and not feel that he is being exploited – on the contrary, considering the publisher's terms generous.

One of the difficulties facing authors is that publishers' contracts vary from firm to firm, and from book to book within each firm. This is neither surprising nor evidence of sharp practice – one of the truisms of the book world is that every book is different. Equally, every publisher is different, and there are good ones and bad ones and vast numbers of them who are just average. Thank God it is so. Publishers will only be alike when they are all State-owned and State-run, which Heaven forfend, when they will probably all be equally bad. You should not expect all publishers to behave the same way and to offer the same terms, any more than you should expect a first novelist to receive the same treatment as one with a worldwide bestselling reputation. Nevertheless, it is all rather confusing.

Moreover, precisely because publishers are perpetually in a buyer's market they have been able, if not to exploit authors outrageously, at least often to be niggardly towards them, and this has perhaps been particularly true in their refusal to share more generously with the author in the rewards of a successful book.

Unless he is consistently in the bestseller class, in which case he or his agent will probably be able easily to obtain a favourable contract, the individual author has little chance of fighting successfully for improved terms, especially since he may not fully understand the wording of the agreement, not to mention the ease with which the publisher can say, "This is our standard contract," with the implication that all his other authors accept it without demur, or even more tellingly, "This is standard practice throughout the trade," a statement which the author will be in no position to contradict. Such a fight can only be won if all authors band together, or if sufficiently influential bodies fight on their behalf. It is for this reason that the Society of Authors and the Writers' Guild have recently produced a form of agreement which they hope to persuade all publishers to accept, setting out the minimum terms for contracts between authors and publishers.

In December 1981 the Publishers Association, after studying the Minimum Terms Agreement, stated that it was not willing to bind its members to observe certain minimum basic terms. This was not wholly unexpected. The Association did, however, acknowledge that "there are inevitably points of legitimate concern, where authors' and publishers' interests may be in conflict, or when, for example, an author or publisher is new and unaware of desirable standards, and the Publishers Association, on behalf of its members, is anxious and willing to do anything within its scope to assist in ensuring good relations between authors and publishers when such situations arise". The Association proposed that a code of practice, giving "firm and clear guidance on points of contention and methods of resolving unforeseen situations", should be agreed and published, and the Society of Authors and the Writers' Guild have expressed their interest in such a code of practice.

In the meantime, the Society of Authors and the Writers' Guild are approaching a number of publishing companies with a view to agreeing minimum terms. I do not know how many publishers will have accepted these terms by the time that you are reading this book. You may think that for any to refuse to do so is incontrovertible evidence of their willingness to continue to exploit authors, since the terms are manifestly no more than fair to those who produce the basic material from which publishers make their money. However, there are arguments on the other side. With the joint permission of the Society of Authors and the Writers' Guild I now reproduce the Minimum Terms Agreement as drafted by them, and I shall then comment on it, clause by clause (except for those points which it seems to me are both self-explanatory and not likely to prove controversial). If in these comments it would appear that I present the publisher's case with particular weight, I would point out that I do so not in any spirit of criticism of the Minimum Terms Agreement, but to warn authors of the possible alterations to the standard terms which their publishers may insist on, and their reasons for resisting the new suggestions. Of course, not all publishers will necessarily object to the same clauses of the MTA. It should also be made clear from the outset that publishers who accept the MTA (or any amended form of it which is also acceptable to the Society of Authors and the Writers' Guild) are not under any obligation to maintain these minima if they are dealing with authors who are not members of the Society of Authors or the Writers' Guild.

See Author's Note on page 123.

MINIMUM TERMS AGREEMENT

AN   AGREEMENT   made   this   day
of   198 between The Society of Authors
and The Writers' Guild of Great Britain of the one part
and   (hereinafter
called   "the   Publishers")   of   the   other   part
                                             WHEREBY
IT IS AGREED AS FOLLOWS

A Scope of Agreement
This Agreement contains the minimum terms and
conditions to be observed in all contracts ("the contract") between the Publishers and all members of the
Society of Authors and all members of the Writers'
Guild (any such members being called "the Author")
in respect of any original literary work published in
hardcover volume form but excluding the following
categories:

1 Illustrated books defined as books which would not
  have been published save for the illustrations.
2 Technical books, manuals, reference works.
3 Textbooks written for the educational market (as
  distinct from general books of an academic or instructional nature).
4 Books involving three or more writers.
5 Plays and poetry.

B Nature of Agreement
1 The terms and conditions of the contract shall be no
  less favourable to the Author nor in any way detract
  from or qualify the terms and conditions specified in
  Section C hereof.
2 This Agreement may be re-negotiated on either
  party giving to the other three months' written
  notice expiring at any time after the fifth anniversary
  hereof.
3 The contract shall contain the words "drafted in
  accordance with the Society of Authors/Writers'
  Guild Minimum Terms Agreement".

C Terms of the Contract between the Author and the Publisher

1 *Delivery & Acceptance of the Typescript*

(a) The Author shall deliver not later than the date specified in the contract one legible copy of the typescript of the work. The contract shall specify the fullest possible details of length, number and type of illustrations, index, etc. The Author shall deliver a script which, in style and content, is professionally competent and fit for publication.

(b) The Publishers shall notify the Author of any changes required in the script within 30 days. Should the Publishers reject the script on the ground that it fails to meet the specifications in (a) above, they shall within 30 days provide the Author with written notice of not less than 250 words in which the grounds for rejecting the script shall be set out in such a manner as to facilitate arbitration under clause 25 below.

(c) The Publishers shall not reject the script for any reason other than its failure to meet the specifications in (a) above.

(d) Should the Author fail to meet the delivery date specified, the Publishers may give the Author six months' notice in writing to deliver the work and should he fail to do so the Publishers shall be entitled to terminate the contract in which event any advance shall be returnable and all rights shall revert to the Author.

2 *Warranty & Indemnity*

The Author shall warrant that the work is an original work, that it has not been published within the territories in which exclusive rights have been granted to the Publishers by the contract, that it does not infringe any existing copyright, and that to the best of the author's knowledge and ability it contains nothing libellous or defamatory.

The Author shall indemnify the Publishers against any loss injury or damage resulting from any breach by the Author (unknown to the Publishers) of the warranty, provided that any legal costs and expenses and any compensation, damages, costs and disbursements shall be paid by the Publishers only on the joint advice of the respective legal advisers of the Author and the Publishers and failing agreement on the advice of Counsel selected and instructed jointly on behalf of the Publishers and the Author. The extent of the Author's indemnity shall not exceed the total moneys received by the Author under the contract.

3 *Copyright Fees & Index*
   (a) The Publishers shall pay any copyright fees for illustrations and/or quotations up to a maximum of £   , any further sum being paid by the Publishers but deducted from the Author's royalties.
   (b) If in the opinion of the Author and the Publishers an index is required but the Author does not wish to undertake the task, the Publishers shall engage a competent indexer to do so and the costs shall be shared equally between the Author and the Publishers, the Author's share being deducted from royalties.

4 *Licence*
   The copyright in the work shall remain the property of the Author who shall grant to the Publishers the sole and exclusive right for a period of ten years from the date of the contract or delivery of the script (whichever is the later) to print, publish and sell the work in volume form and to sub-license the rights specified in Clauses 13, 14, 15, 16 and 17 (a) hereof as may be agreed in the contract. Except in the case of anthology and quotation rights, if the Publishers wish to enter into any such sub-licence, they shall obtain the consent of the Author (such consent not to be unreasonably withheld or delayed) supplying him with a copy of the sub-licence before it is signed. If the work is in print (as defined in Clause 23(b) hereof) at the end of ten years after delivery of the typescript, the Publishers shall have first refusal to enter into a further contract with the Author.

5 *Publishers' Undertaking to Publish*
   Provided that the work meets the specification in Clause 1(a) above, the Publishers shall publish the work at their own expense and risk in a first edition consisting of the number of copies named in approximate terms in the contract within twelve months (unless otherwise agreed in writing) of delivery of the typescript and any other material

specified in accordance with Clause 1. Should the Publishers fail to comply with their undertaking, the advance stipulated in Clause 10 hereof (or any balance unpaid) shall be paid to the Author together with such additional amount as may be awarded under Clause 25 hereof as compensation for such failure by the Publishers.

6 *Production*

    (a) All details as to the manner of production and publication and the number and destination of free copies shall be under the control of the Publishers who undertake to produce the book to a high standard.

    (b) The Publishers shall obtain the Author's approval of copy editing, blurb, catalogue copy, number and type of illustrations, jacket design and publication date, such approval not to be unreasonably withheld or delayed.

    (c) No changes in the title or text shall be made by the Publishers without the Author's written consent.

    (d) Within ten days of publication the Publishers shall inform the Author of the number of copies printed and the number and destination of free copies distributed.

    (e) Within thirty days of publication the Publishers shall return to the Author the typescript of the work.

    (f) The Publishers shall ensure that the provisions contained in (b) and (c) above are included in any contract for sub-licensed editions of the work in the English language.

7 *Approval of Final Edited Script and Correction of Proofs*

    (a) The Author shall be sent for approval a copy of the final edited script at least 14 days before it goes to the printers.

    (b) The Author shall be sent two complete sets of proofs of the work and proofs of the illustrations and captions and notes on the jacket. The Author shall correct and return one set of proofs to the Publishers within 14 days. The Author shall bear the cost of proof corrections (other than printers' or Publishers' errors) in excess of 15% of the cost of composition, such cost to be deducted from royalties.

8 *Marketing*
The Publishers shall use their best endeavours to market the work effectively and shall, in particular, despatch review copies at least one month before the publication date, include and describe correctly the work in their catalogue, and do everything they reasonably can to ensure that copies are ready for sale in all leading bookshops by publication day.

9 *Copyright Notice and Credit to the Author*
A copyright notice in the form © followed by the Author's name and the year of publication shall be printed on all copies of the work and the Author's name shall appear prominently on the jacket, binding and title page of the work and in all publicity material. The Publishers shall ensure that an identical copyright notice appears in all sub-licensed editions of the work.

10 *Advance*
(a) The Publishers shall pay the Author an advance against royalties which shall be calculated as follows:
   (i)   On account of the Publishers' own editions: not less than 65% of the Author's estimated receipts from the sale of the projected first printing (if the Publishers' turnover is not less than £   per annum); and
   (ii) On account of any rights granted under clauses 13, 14, 15 & 16: a sum additional to that under (i) above, to be negotiated between the Author and the Publishers and to be itemized separately both in the contract and the account statements to be rendered to the Author.
(b) In the case of a non-commissioned work half the advance shall be paid on signature of the contract and half within one year of signature or on publication whichever is the sooner.
(c) In the case of a commissioned work the advance shall be paid either
   (i)   one third on signature of the contract, one third on delivery of the typescript and one third within one year of delivery of the typescript or on publication whichever is the sooner; or
   (ii) one half on signature of the contract and one half on delivery of the typescript.

    (d) Except in the case of termination of the contract pursuant to clause 1 (d) above, the advance shall be non-returnable and shall be paid in full.

    (e) Within ten days of publication the Publishers shall pay to the Author such sum as may be required to bring the advance payment up to the 65% of the Author's receipts from the sale of the entire first printing.

11 *Royalties*

    (a) *On home market sales in the UK and Irish Republic and on overseas sales at discounts of less than 45%*
    10% of the British published price on the first 2,500 copies, 12½% on the next 2,500 copies, and 15% thereafter

    (b) *On overseas sales (other than to the USA) at discounts of 45% or more*
    5% of the British published price on the first 2,500 copies, 6¼% on the next 2,500 copies, and 7½% thereafter

    (c) *English language editions published overseas (other than US editions)*
    The Publishers shall pay to the Author a royalty to be agreed on all copies of any edition in the English language produced and published outside the United Kingdom (other than the USA) either by themselves or by arrangement with another publisher.

    (d) Reduced royalties shall not be paid on any reprint unless otherwise agreed in writing.

    (e) No proportion of royalties due to the Author shall be reserved against return copies.

    (f) *Cheap and other hardback editions*
    The Publishers shall pay to the Author a royalty to be agreed on any hardback edition published at less than two-thirds of the original published price and also on any "special" hardback edition under their imprint, e.g. an educational or large print edition.

12 *Remainders & Surplus Stock*
If not less than two years after first publication the Publishers

    (a) wish to sell off copies at a reduced price or as a remainder; or

    (b) wish to destroy surplus bound copies

they shall notify the Author accordingly. In the case

of (a) the Publishers shall pay the Author 10% of the net receipts and shall give him the option to purchase copies at the remainder price. In the case of (b) the Author shall have the right to obtain free copies within 28 days of the notification.

13 *Paperbacks*
   (a) Should the Publishers publish a paperback edition under their own imprint or under that of an associated company they shall pay to the Author on all sales in the home market & overseas including the USA 7½% of the British published price on the first 20,000 copies and 10% thereafter.
   (b) Should the Publishers sub-license paperback rights to an independent paperback publisher, all moneys accruing under such sub-licence shall be divided in the proportion 60% to the Author and 40% to the Publishers on the first £5,000 accruing under the sub-licence, and 70% to the Author and 30% to the Publishers thereafter.

14 *Bookclub and Digest Rights*
   Should the Publishers sub-license simultaneous or reprint bookclub rights or the right of condensation in volume form they shall pay the Author as follows:
   (a) On bound copies or sheets sold to the bookclub:
       50% of net receipts (being the difference between the sale price and the cost of manufacture) up to £5,000 and 60% on all receipts thereafter. In the event of such a sale the Publishers shall inform the Author of the gross amount received from the bookclub and the cost of manufacture.
   (b) On copies manufactured by the bookclub:
       60% of the Publishers' receipts up to £5,000 and 70% thereafter
   (c) On copies sold to a bookclub owned or partly owned by the Publishers or one of their associated companies:
       7½% of the bookclub price.

15 *United States Rights*
   (a) If the Author grants to the Publishers US rights in the work, they shall make every effort to

arrange the publication of an American edition of the work on a royalty basis. The Publishers shall retain not more than 15% of the proceeds from any such edition inclusive of any sub-agent's commission. Should the Publishers fail to negotiate publication of an American edition on a royalty basis, but obtain an offer for an edition at a price inclusive of the Author's remuneration, they shall pay the Author not less than 12½% of their net receipts.

(b) If the Author retains US rights but the Publishers agree to act as his agent for the sale of these rights, US publication shall be covered by a separate contract between the Author and the American publishers. The Publishers shall retain as an agency commission not more than 15% of the proceeds from any such edition inclusive of any sub-agent's commission.

16 *Translation Rights*

(a) If the Author grants to the Publishers translation rights in the work they shall retain not more than 20% of the proceeds from any foreign-language edition inclusive of any sub-agent's commission.

(b) If the Author retains translation rights but the publishers agree to act as his agent for the sale of these rights, any foreign-language edition of the work shall be covered by a separate contract between the Author and the foreign-language publishers. The Publishers shall retain as an agency commission not more than 20% of the proceeds from any such edition inclusive of any sub-agent's commission.

17 *Subsidiary Rights*

(a) If the Author grants to the Publishers an exclusive licence to handle the following rights on his behalf the Publishers shall pay to the Author the following percentages of the proceeds:

(i)   Second, i.e. post-volume publication serial rights   80%
(ii) Anthology & quotation rights   60%
(iii) Condensation rights   75%
(iv) Strip cartoon rights   75%

(b) The following rights shall be expressly reserved for the Author together with any rights not specified above:

First serial, one-shot periodical, film and
dramatic, TV and radio dramatization, TV and
radio readings, reprography, merchandizing,
video and sound recording, Public Lending.

18 *Author's Copies*
The Author shall receive on publication 12 presentation copies of the work and shall have the right
to purchase further copies at the lowest trade price
for personal use. Should a paperback edition be
issued under clause 13(a), the Author shall be entitled to 20 presentation copies.

19 *Accounts*
   (a) The Publishers shall make up accounts at six-
       monthly intervals in each year and shall render
       such accounts and pay all moneys due to the
       Author within three months thereof.
   (b) Moneys due to the Author under either Clause
       10(a) (i) or Clause 10(a) (ii) shall not be withheld
       on account of an unearned advance under the
       other of these two sub-clauses. Any sum of
       £100 or more due to the Author in respect of
       sub-licensed rights shall be paid to the Author
       within one month of receipt provided the ad-
       vance under Clause 10(a) (ii) has been earned.
   (c) Each statement of account shall report the
       number of copies printed, the number of free
       copies distributed, the number of copies sold
       during the previous accounting period, the tot-
       al sales to date, the list price, the royalty rate,
       the amount of royalties, the number of re-
       turned copies, the gross amount received pur-
       suant to each licence granted by the Publishers,
       and itemized deductions. Each statement of
       account shall be accompanied by copies of
       statements received from sub-licensed pub-
       lishers.
   (d) The Publishers shall make no deductions from
       moneys due to the Author other than those
       provided for herein. In the event of late pay-
       ment, the Publishers shall pay interest on
       moneys overdue at the rate of 3% above the
       base rate of the major clearing banks.
   (e) The Author or his authorized representative
       shall have the right upon written request to
       examine the Publishers' books of account in so
       far as they relate to the work, which examina-

tion shall be at the cost of the Author unless errors exceeding 2% of the total sums paid to the Author shall be found to his disadvantage in which case the costs shall be paid by the Publishers.

20 *Actions for Infringement*

If either the Author or the Publishers consider the copyright in the work has been infringed both parties shall join in any legal proceedings and the party initiating such proceedings shall pay all costs and expenses and indemnify the other. Any moneys which shall be recovered in respect of any such infringement of copyright shall after deduction of all costs and expenses be divided equally between Author and Publishers.

21 *Revised Editions*

The work shall not be revised or re-issued in altered or expanded form without the Author's consent. If the Author and the Publishers agree that the Author shall undertake revisions or provide new material for a new edition, this work shall be undertaken subject to an agreed advance against royalties to the Author. No third party shall be engaged to revise or add to the work without the Author's written consent.

22 *Assignment*

The Publishers shall not assign the rights granted to them in the contract or the benefit thereof without the Author's written consent.

23 *Termination*

(a) If the Publishers fail to fulfil or comply with any of the provisions of the contract within one month after notification from the Author of such failure or if they go into liquidation or have a Receiver appointed, the contract shall automatically terminate and all rights granted by it shall revert to the Author.

(b) If after all editions of the work published under their own imprint are out of print or off the market the Publishers have not within six months of a written request from the Author issued a new edition or impression of at least 1,500 copies (unless a lesser number of copies be mutually agreed) the contract shall terminate and all rights granted shall revert to the

Author. The work shall be considered to be out of print for the purposes of the contract if fewer than 12 copies of an edition under the Publishers' imprint are shown to have been sold in any statement of account or if fewer than 50 copies remain in stock.

Termination under (a) or (b) above shall be without prejudice to:

(i) any sub-licences properly granted by the Publishers during the currency of the contract, and

(ii) any claims which the Author may have for moneys due at the time of such termination, and

(iii) any claims which the Author may have against the Publishers in respect of breaches by the Publishers of the terms of the contract.

24 *Advertisements*

The Publishers and the publishers of any sub-licensed edition shall not insert within the work or on its cover or dust jacket any advertisement other than for their own works without the Author's consent.

25 *Disputes*

Any dispute arising in connection with the contract shall be referred to a joint committee composed of a representative of the Society of Authors, a representative of the Writers' Guild and two representatives appointed by the Publishers but not connected with their company, whose unanimous decision shall be binding. Failing unanimous agreement, the dispute shall be referred to a single arbitrator appointed by the above named parties and the decision of the arbitrator shall be binding. Failing agreement on the choice of a single arbitrator, the dispute shall be referred to the London Court of Arbitration under its rules.

26 *Option*

The Author shall not grant the Publishers an option or first refusal on any of his future works.

APPENDIX A. PAPERBACK AGREEMENT

Where the work is originally published in paperback form by the Publishers the minimum terms and conditions shall be the same as those set out in the hard-cover Agreement except that the following clauses shall be substituted:

Clause 11　Royalties
  (a)　*on all sales in the home market and overseas including the USA*
    7½% of the British published price on the first 20,000 copies and 10% of the British published price thereafter
  (b)　reduced royalties shall not be paid on any re-print unless otherwise agreed in writing
  (c)　no proportion of royalties due to the Author shall be reserved against return copies

Clause 13　Hardcover Editions
  (a)　Should the Publishers publish a hardcover edition under their own imprint or under that of an associated company the Publishers shall pay to the Author the following royalties:
    (i)　*on home market sales in the UK and Irish Republic and on overseas sales at discounts of less than 45%*
      10% of the British published price on the first 2,500 copies, 12½% on the next 2,500 copies, and 15% thereafter
    (ii)　*on overseas sales (other than the USA) at discounts of 45% or more*
      5% of the British published price on the first 2,500 copies, 6¼% on the next 2,500 copies, and 7½% thereafter
  (b)　Should the Publishers sub-license hardcover rights to an independent hardcover publisher, all moneys accruing under such a sub-licence shall be divided in the proportion 80% to the Author and 20% to the Publishers.

The first point to be made is that however just the terms in the agreement may be (and there is no doubt that any dispassionate analyst would find it extremely difficult to argue against their fairness or to claim that they would result in over-generous rewards being paid to authors), the extra money will have to come from somewhere. To say glibly that it can come from publishers' profits is to ignore the difficulties which publishers face at present, and which are not by any means solely the result of national or worldwide depression, and indeed to believe that all publishing houses are little goldmines, which is manifestly not true. No, the money will have to come from the public, as it always does when any group of workers improves its pay. Unfortunately, however, that may be dangerous, for books are already regarded as expensive and to many people are undoubtedly a luxury item. Higher prices may mean smaller print quantities, which would certainly mean fewer books accepted for publication. Wherever the additional money is to come from, the effect of the MTA is bound to be that publishers will look even more carefully than in the past at their future projects, and if they have to bear all or a part of the extra costs, then they will sign up fewer books and will have less capital available for investment in long-term commitments.

The second important thing to say is that any agreement must to some extent be a matter of give and take. The writing and publishing of a book is almost always an unpredictable business. All kinds of problems may occur, which demand some relaxation of the terms of the agreement, and although a contract between a publisher and an author is a legal document, meaning, if it is well drawn, exactly what it says, and to be strictly interpreted, it is my view that any publisher or author who refused to amend it in any detail according to changing circumstances would be a fool. But of course, before either side can give or take, it is quite essential that there should be a clear understanding between them of what the change entails and why it is necessary. This is one of the reasons why it is so important to establish a personal relationship with your publisher, and if possible a friendship, and just as the publisher should try to understand the author's problems and something of his circumstances, so the author should try to understand something about the publisher's work and the difficulties that he encounters. It is worth remembering that though your publishing house is a business, it is staffed by human beings, and human behaviour can often be extremely mysterious. The more you understand of what makes your publisher tick, the easier it will be to reach agreement with him. If each side understands the other, there can be no argument, but only a discussion, and it is much easier to settle a discussion than an argument.

Now to go through the terms of the agreement set out on the previous pages, picking up those points with which your publisher may disagree, beginning at Section C.

Clause 1 Delivery and Acceptance of the Typescript

(a) and (c) Most publishers ask for two copies of the type-script, which enables more than one function to be performed at once on the book, as described in Chapter 4. The expense and trouble to the author in making an extra carbon copy is, the publisher will say, minimal, whereas for him it is both expensive and time-consuming.

Note in sub-clause (a) the sentence, "The Author shall deliver a script which, in style and content, is professionally competent and fit for publication." Legally it might be extremely difficult to define exactly what "professionally competent" and "fit for publication" mean, but the spirit of the words is crystal clear, and if all authors abided by them, there would be far fewer publishers wanting to include a provision for "acceptance" of the typescript in their contracts. In its *Quick Guide to Publishing Contracts*, the Society of Authors points out that if a clause is included which makes the publisher's obligation to publish subject to his acceptance of the book (and this is sometimes merely implied in that part of the advance is "payable on delivery and acceptance"), then the agreement has been turned into nothing more than a promise to consider the book for publication, and it strongly advises all authors not to accept an "acceptance" clause. It argues that publishers have the means, by insisting on receiving detailed synopses and specimen chapters before commissioning a book, of satisfying themselves that the author is competent to write it. However, believe it or not, not all the rogues are on the publishing side of the book business, and every publisher can cite cases in which, despite the most careful precautions and sometimes involving well-established authors, books turned out to be unpublishable when delivered. Publishers really do feel that they need some protection against the incompetent or unscrupulous author. "Ah, well," the proponents of the MTA will say, "if the publisher and the author are in dispute concerning the quality of the typescript, the matter can be referred to arbitration." But the publisher would not have much confidence in arbitration – in matters of opinion, the creative individual is far more likely to be supported than the faceless, middleman limited company, which is assumed to be well able to afford the advance which it is cruelly demanding should be returned.

In any case, it is fair to point out that the majority of books which have an acceptance clause do eventually get published by the house whose contract it is. By including the word "acceptance" the publisher may have given himself a loophole allowing him not to go ahead, but that is not his intention. He wants the opportunity of improving the type-script and if it is not acceptable to him when first delivered will usually spare little effort to get the author himself or (with the author's permission) his editors to knock it into shape. It shouldn't be necessary, if all authors could be relied on to deliver a typescript which could not be improved on, but few could make that claim for their work.

If the concept of "acceptance" is to go, then publishers will argue that they will have to take fewer risks in commissioning books. That may mean fewer commissions. However, even if that is the end result, authors should do their utmost to resist the inclusion of an acceptance clause in a contract, because it can be very dangerous, especially in these days of the cutting back of lists, changes of policy, and the sudden disappearance of editors. Sub-clause (c) should really provide adequate protection for the publisher, and if he does not consider that "the script, in style and content, is professionally competent and fit for publication", then the onus should be on him to *prove* that it is not.

(b) In an ideal world, publishers would always notify the author of any changes required within thirty days. However, many things can conspire to make this deadline very difficult to meet: holidays, the need for specialist readings (including the time taken for the book to get to and from the specialist reader through Her Majesty's mails), and the simple pressure of other work. But this is a matter for understanding on both sides – provided of course that the publisher explains within the thirty days why a delay is necessary.

If the publisher does ask for alterations, authors should

listen carefully. Publishers don't usually suggest changes for changes' sake, but in the hope of improving the book and its sales. Accept the criticisms if you can, but, as I have said elsewhere, fight for your work if you really believe that you are right. Most good editors recognize that there is a point beyond which the competent author should not be pushed – it is his book, not the editor's, and he should be allowed the final say.

Clause 2 Warranty and Indemnity

Publishers' contracts vary widely in the scope of their warranty and indemnity clauses, which are often a cause of strife, and some houses, prompted by their lawyers, insist firmly on using their own form of this clause. In such cases, beware especially of the mention of the author's responsibility for indemnifying the publisher against expenses resulting from any *threat* of action, even if it is not pursued. There is really no reason why, if he has not breached his warranty, the author should be expected to bear any such costs, which should surely be part of the publisher's normal expenses.

Some publishers also include a warranty against obscenity or blasphemy in this clause and may reserve the right to remove any libellous, defamatory, obscene or blasphemous passages from the book. Naturally, however, they should consult the author and obtain his consent first.

Note, in the MTA version of the clause, the phrase "unknown to the publisher". If the publisher is aware that the book is libellous and still proceeds with publication, then all responsibility should be transferred from the author to him. But it would be important, I think, for the author in such circumstances to obtain from the publisher a statement in writing accepting the responsibility.

The idea that the author's liability should be limited to the amounts paid to him under the agreement may not find ready acceptance, and it seems to me a rather curious provision, especially if the sums paid to the author are minimal, as they may be for a book with very modest sales expectations. Of course, publishers are usually better equipped than their impecunious authors to meet a demand for heavy libel damages, and most of them realize perfectly well that despite the indemnity clause they have little hope of recovering their total costs from the author, who is rarely wealthy enough to pay up.

Clause 3 Copyright Fees and Index

This clause is almost certainly negotiable, depending on the nature of the work. Sometimes the publisher will agree to make a contribution to such costs, either by increasing the advance paid (a bad and unhelpful idea) or in a separate lump sum. Publishers may want to change that part of the clause which allows for the deduction of any sums payable by the author from his royalties. In theory, this should be satisfactory to both parties, but if the advance is not earned and no royalties are payable, it certainly won't be acceptable to the publisher, since it means that he has to pay all the costs involved. It is extremely important that agreement should be reached between the author and his publisher regarding the payment of fees, especially those for illustrations, and it is advisable to have a separate document (a letter is adequate) setting out the arrangement in full and unambiguous detail, so that neither party is in doubt about where they stand, and the arguments over these fees which so frequently occur between authors and publishers can be avoided.

Clause 4 Licence

This is perhaps the most controversial clause in the MTA. Hardcover publishers have been in the habit of buying rights for the full term of copyright. The Society of Authors and the Writers' Guild argue that hardcover publishers normally grant sub-licences for a limited period only, and what is sauce for the goose should be sauce for the gander too. Given goodwill on both sides, it should not be considered an unreasonable proposition, but publishers may fear being held to ransom by successful authors at the end of the ten-year period when they want to renew the licence.

It is entirely reasonable that the author should receive copies of sub-licence agreements, but some publishers will say that it could cause unwarrantable delays, especially since complex explanations might sometimes be necessary, to show the author the agreement before signature.

The clause is silent about what happens to sub-licences at the end of the ten-year period of the main licence, and publishers will want to clarify that situation, especially since otherwise their ability to grant a sub-licence several years after their own original publication might be jeopardized.

Clause 5 Publishers' Undertaking to Publish

If the book is of a very complex nature, with perhaps a great many illustrations or special setting, or if to comply with the twelve months' limit it would have to be published at a very unsuitable time of the year, or if the publisher is prevented from bringing the book out by circumstances beyond his control (for instance, by a strike in the printing industry), then the publisher might require a longer period between delivery of the book and publication. This is, however, provided for by the words "unless otherwise agreed in writing", and authors will no doubt be reasonable in this respect if the circumstances are explained to them.

One has heard too many sad tales of publication delays to believe that this clause, in some form or other, is not necessary, and authors should insist on the publisher making a reasonable but definite commitment to publish within a given period. Most publishers are actually eager to publish the books on their list as soon as they can so that they can recoup any money they have already spent on it – but some can nevertheless be very dilatory.

Clause 6 Production

(b) Not so many years ago it was almost unheard of for an author to be consulted in such matters as catalogue copy and jacket design. More recently, the better publishers have realized that authors can actually be a help rather than a hindrance in such matters. If your publisher does not accept this clause, he is probably less eager to maintain his "I know best" attitude than anxious over the possibility of long delays and acrimonious arguments. As with so many things, provided the author does not unreasonably withhold his approval, there should be no need for conflict.

(d) Publishers have often been remarkably reluctant in the past to inform authors of the number of copies printed of their books, but there seems to be no good reason why this information should not be given. As for the number of free copies sent out and their destination, I think many publishers will find this a chore which would result in information of comparatively little use to the author, especially as many free copies are in fact sent out longer than ten days after publication.

Clause 7 Approval of Final Edited Script and Correction of Proofs

The more usual percentage of the composition cost above which the author pays for corrections is 10%. Prudent authors will avoid any likelihood of a charge by making sure that the final typescript is as perfect as possible. In the case of topical books where changes have to be made to ensure that the book is up to date, special arrangements regarding alterations in proof should be made with the publisher. Again the publisher may not like the idea of deducting the author's proof correcting costs from possibly non-existent royalties, and his argument would not seem unreasonable.

Clause 8 Marketing

The intention of this clause is excellent, but it contains a number of phrases which defy legal definition, such as "best endeavours" and "effective" and "everything they reasonably can". Who is to say exactly what these fine words mean? Of course the publisher who does not do all these things as a matter of course is a fool anyway.

Clause 10 Advance

(a) (i) and (ii) The idea of relating the advance to the print quantity is a good one, though there may be some difficulty in that publishers will naturally tend to base their figures on low sales projections and perhaps with a bias towards those, such as export sales, on which lower royalties are payable. Publishers will also be quick to point out that their receipts from sales of their books to retailers and wholesalers take on average three months to come in, and will argue that they are justified in asking authors to wait until the moneys have come in before they are paid.

It is also very reasonable to ask that a separate advance should cover moneys from sources other than royalties on the publisher's original edition, but publishers may be reluctant to commit themselves to substantial advance payments for subsidiary rights, arguing that the markets are so unstable that they cannot be certain of making the sales. Indeed the effect of these two sub-clauses, as that of the MTA as a whole, could be, by making publishers much more cautious than in the past, to make it more difficult for authors to get their books accepted.

Clause 11 Royalties

(a) Royalties offered to authors in the past have varied enormously, some not rising from a basic rate at all, others jumping at widely differing points. Some publishers will argue that to increase royalties after 2,500 copies and again after 5,000 copies will mean that the retail price of books will have to be increased, with a possible reduction of sales as a result. For instance, a 2½% increase in royalty on a book priced at £6.95 requires an increase in retail price of 25p to cover that royalty, without increasing the publisher's gross or net profit, where the bookseller's discount is 35%. Of course, it is not quite as simple as that, since the higher retail price would give the publisher a better return on those copies on which the lower royalty rate was applicable, but nevertheless publishers will argue that there is considerable consumer resistance to any increase in book prices and that this scale of royalties attacks them when they are most vulnerable, that is to say in the case of books for which a minimum print run and sale has to be envisaged. The counter argument is that once home sales have reached 2,500, given that there will also be a reasonable quantity of export sales, the print quantity will be high enough for the origination costs to be spread sufficiently so that the publisher can afford the extra payment to the author without either reducing his own profit or increasing the retail price of the book.

Some publishers nowadays are proposing to pay royalties on their net receipts rather than on the published price of the book. There are considerable advantages to the publisher in this method, since it so greatly simplifies his royalty accounting, and also allows him freedom to change the discounts at which he sells to certain of his customers, thus achieving, he hopes, larger sales (his argument here being that by paying authors royalties on the published price he is sometimes prevented from selling books at high discounts, whereas if the royalty is calculated on the price received, the author may earn less per copy on those sales, but at least the books will be sold, which otherwise they would not have been). The important point to note is that the royalty paid on the publisher's net receipts must be substantially higher than normal royalty scales. If the publisher's average discount to his customers is 40%, then a 16.6% royalty on net receipts would be necessary to be the equivalent of a 10% royalty on the published price. Incidentally, if the Net Book Agreement were ever abolished, the publisher could well argue that a royalty based on his net receipts would be much fairer than one based on a recommended retail price which no one was observing.

(b) Many publishers will argue that a substantial number of their export sales are made at a discount of 40%, but that they should still have the benefit of paying a reduced royalty on such sales because of the extra cost of achieving them, the additional freight costs and the fact that payment from overseas customers takes a very long time to come in, with the result that the publisher's capital is tied up longer than is the case with home sales and his interest expenses (since almost all publishers live on borrowed money) are increased.

The idea of expressing export royalties as a percentage of the British published price, and especially the suggestion of a sliding scale of such royalties, may be resisted. Publishers often prefer a percentage (usually 10%) of their net receipts. The royalty on the published price is to be preferred. There are also some cases (for instance, a book which is expected to sell very substantial quantities in Australia) where it is possible for authors to secure a royalty based on the overseas retail price rather than the British retail price. Since overseas prices are usually very much higher, this may be very advantageous. Note that this is not what is referred to in Clause 11 (c), which is a separate edition.

(d) Many publisher's agreements at present contain a clause allowing for a reduced royalty to be paid on small reprints. Even reprints have heavy origination costs, and if on the first printing of a book the author's royalties have reached one of the higher levels, that royalty rate may make the economics of a small reprint quite unhealthy for the publisher. Your publisher may tell you that he will be unable to reprint at all unless you will take a reduced royalty. Sometimes the argument is reasonable, but the publisher must be prepared to reveal his figures quite openly to you and to give you a convincing explanation of why the reduction in royalty is essential.

(e) This clause may cause some difficulties. Increasingly, books go out to wholesalers and retailers on a "sale or return" basis. Such books are entered in the publisher's ledgers as sales, but may be nothing of the sort, since the customers have the right to return for credit the copies that they have not sold after a given period. Supposing a publisher has sent out 1,000 copies of a book on sale or return; they are counted as full sales and royalties on them paid to the author at the end of the accounting period; but in the subsequent royalty period, 250 of those books are returned for credit, which means that the author has been paid royalties on books which have not been sold. This will not matter if a further 250 firm sales are made, because the returns can be offset against them, but often no more sales are made. Equally, it would not matter if the author were prepared to return any royalties paid to him for sale or return books which turned out not to be firm sales, but in practice, though the advance is supposed to be the only non-returnable payment made to an author, publishers have long come to accept that any moneys paid to an author are lost to them for ever. If authors could be persuaded to salt away their own reserves against returns, which could earn interest for them until it became clear whether or not the money was theirs to keep, and if it could be guaranteed that they would make any payments due, there would be little problem. Most authors, however, seem to be chronically hard up, and usually spend all their royalties as soon as they receive them, if not before.

The problem of returns occurs particularly in the paperback business, and for some years now several paperback publishers have been making admittedly arbitrary reserves against returns, paying royalties on only a proportion of the books despatched until the passage of time has revealed whether those sales are genuine or not. The customary process has been to make the reserve not only on sales accounted for in the first royalty period, when the bulk of the sales are made and when the potential of the book in question has had little chance of being tested, but to carry that reserve for two or more subsequent royalty periods. If this new clause is accepted it may mean that some publishers will be forced into differentiating in their ledgers between firm sales and sale or return sales, paying royalties only on the former. The arguments are readily understandable on both sides: why should the author have to wait for payment on an arbitrarily reserved proportion of the sales if they all turn out to be firm, but why should the publisher pay royalties on sales which turn out to be non-existent?

Clause 12 Remainders and Surplus Stock

Many publishers will argue that a large number of the books on the list which they have to remainder or pulp can be seen to be unmitigated disasters within six months of publication, and that they should be free to dispose of them in a lesser period than two years from publication. Authors will not unnaturally feel that this is to give the books little chance. Compromises can sometimes be reached.

The payment of a royalty on remainders sold at manufacturing cost or less has been mooted for some time, and resisted by the majority of publishers, who say that they should not be asked to add to their losses on these copies by paying the author a royalty. Since the books eventually reach the public, it seems quite unfair that the author should receive no reward at all for such sales. The solution must surely be for publishers to force up the price of their remainder sales so that they can afford to pay the author a royalty.

Clause 13 Paperbacks

For many years, it was standard practice for the publisher of the hardcover edition to retain 50% of all the royalties received on a sub-licensed paperback edition, and his arguments for doing so were that if he had not published the book in the first place, the paperback edition would not have appeared; that he had invested money in building up the author's reputation, publicizing his book, securing reviews for it, and so on, and that if he had not done so the paperback publisher would not have been interested in it; that the growth of paperback sales had eradicated the hardcover publisher's ability to sell cheap editions of the hardcover book, making his initial risk that much greater; and that without a substantial share of the paperback income he would be unable to publish many new books, and especially new fiction (and it is certainly true today that many publishers would go out of business even more rapidly, or at least curtail their lists, if they could not rely on the income that they receive from paperback and other subsidiary rights). Gradually, however, over recent years, thanks largely to the concerted action of authors' agents, the concept of the invariable 50/50 split has been eroded, and publishers have survived and have even been known to admit that, particularly when large sums of money are involved, the author is entitled to a higher proportion of the subsidiary income. Some publishers may, however, still wish to negotiate lower shares for the author on books which they consider to have been particularly expensive or risky for them to produce. On paperbacks published under their own imprint or that of an associated company publishers will want to negotiate a lower royalty on export sales.

Clause 14 Bookclub and Digest Rights

(a) Most publishers have been in the habit of paying the author a royalty (usually 3¾% of the bookclub's price to its members) on bound copies or sheets sold to a bookclub, claiming that the cost of manufacture and the profit that they make on the deal is none of the author's business. Why should the author want to know anyway? So that he can make sure that he is not being cheated. Anything which affects the money due to him *is* the author's business.

(b) The remarks concerning Clause 13 (b) apply here too.

Clause 15 United States Rights

(a) Publishers have usually taken a percentage (usually 20%) of *net* receipts, i.e. after any sub-agent's commission has been paid, and to pay the sub-agent's commission themselves will have the effect of reducing their cut of these rights to 10%, a figure which they will say does not cover their expenses in selling the rights.

On the sale of an edition inclusive of the author's royalty, 10% of the net receipts has usually been paid, and any change has been downwards rather than upwards. It has to be said that the fluctuations of the exchange rate have often made it extremely difficult to sell editions to American publishers, and British publishers have been forced to trim their prices to extremely narrow margins. Even 12½% of the net receipts may be a remarkably small reward for the author, often meaning that he will receive something like 5% of the British retail price on copies sold in the United States at a much higher retail price. However, it is frequently a case of accepting that or nothing.

Clause 16 Translation Rights

(a) Again, there may be some difficulty in getting publishers to agree to the payment of the author's share exclusive of sub-agent's commission.

Clause 17 Subsidiary Rights

The percentages shown here are again higher than it has been normal practice for hardcover publishers to pay. As for the reservation of rights listed in Clause 17 (b), if the author has an agent this arrangement will be expected by the publisher and the agent (if he is a good one) will effectively look after the author's interests in those fields. If, however, the author has no agent, he may be well advised to allow the publisher to handle those rights for him, since the publisher will probably be better equipped than he is himself to deal with them. The percentages that the author receives from such rights should be high – mostly 90%. Note that among the rights to be retained by the author is Public Lending; some publishers may try to take a share of PLR receipts.

Clause 18 Author's Copies

Standard practice has been for the author to receive six copies only. From the publisher's point of view, the addition of a further six free copies is one of the cheapest things he can do to keep his author happy. Some publishers will prefer to specify the price at which authors can purchase additional copies, and authors may themselves prefer this to the vagueness of "the lowest trade price", which phrase might be expected to cover the very low prices at which publishers sell copies of their editions to bookclubs – an idea of which any publisher will quickly disabuse his authors, pointing out that bookclub deals come under subsidiary rights and not normal trade sales. It seems to me not unreasonable that the author should receive at least a 40% discount, and preferably 50%, but it has to be remembered that you receive a royalty on your books when you buy them from the publisher, which effectively lowers the price you pay for them. Publishers may also wish to add to this clause the usual wording prohibiting the author from re-selling copies purchased for his personal use (but see p. 157).

Clause 19 Accounts

(c) Few publishers include all these details on their royalty statements, and some may argue that to do so will only make their task of producing the statements on time more difficult. But at the moment many send out statements which are difficult to understand and contain a minimum of information, and some raising of the overall standard is needed.

(d) Many authors have been understandably irritated by publishers' lateness in submitting royalty statements and making the payments due. The three, or sometimes four months' interval between the end of an accounting period and the issuance of royalty statements should be adequate for even the most complex of publishing lists, and some penalty for late delivery seems fair.

Clause 22 Assignment

Some publishers include in the preamble to their agreements some such wording as "Rows & Crowne Ltd. (hereinafter called 'the Publishers' which expression shall where the context admits include the Publishers' executors, administrators and assigns or successors in business as the case may be)". The present clause is much preferable from the author's point of view, since it should not be possible for the publisher to assign his rights to a third party to whom the author might have reasonable objections.

Clause 23 Termination

In some cases publishers may require more than one month after notification from the author to rectify a failure, and the author should clearly be co-operative in this respect, provided that the publisher can explain the delay satisfactorily and show that he is making good the failure within the shortest possible time.

A well-drawn termination clause is very necessary in all agreements between an author and a publisher. It should be specific regarding the reversion of rights to the author, but so many different circumstances can attach to a book that it is advisable, if termination takes place, to insist that the publisher should state in writing exactly what the situation is (for example, which rights have reverted to the author, which sub-licences are still in existence and how moneys accruing from them will be dealt with, and so on).

Clause 24 Advertisements

In the years before the Second World War it was not unusual for publishers to sell space in their books to advertisers, and it seems to me that they may be driven to do so again in order to subsidize their publications. It is to be hoped that any advertisements· accepted by the publisher would be in good taste and would not be such as to upset the readers of the book or in any way to damage the author's reputation, in which case the author would surely not withhold his consent unreasonably.

Clause 26 Option

The majority of publishers' contracts carry an option clause. If it refers to the terms on which the publisher will be able to buy the author's next book in specific detail, or more usually uses a phrase like "on the same terms and conditions as the present agreement", it is legally binding. Few authors should agree to such a clause, which can clearly be very damaging to their interests. The option "on terms to be agreed" is far less dangerous, since it commits the author only to the submission of his next work for the publisher's consideration and leaves him free to refuse the publisher's offer if he wishes to do so. In practice, publishers should *earn* the right to see the author's next book. If they have behaved well towards him, and especially if they have made a success of the previous book, the author will probably wish to continue to be published by the same firm, and in such a case the publisher is indeed entitled to expect loyalty from his author. Some authors change publishers with alarming regularity, and one may wonder whether the reasons for their dissatisfaction lie more with them than with their publishers. If you are unhappy with your publisher and seek a change, you could easily jump out of the frying pan into the fire, so do be sure first that your complaints against your present publisher are justified and are not likely to arise again when you go to another house. No publisher is perfect, and authors should realize that. No author is perfect, either.

The clauses in the MTA on which I have not commented are both self-explanatory and unlikely in my view to cause much if any friction between author and publisher. In general, the effect of this agreement is not merely to protect authors' rights, but also to increase fairly substantially their rewards. Except in the case of major bestsellers, few people would argue that authors are at present well paid, nor could it be said that the provisions of the MTA are unjustified, but let me repeat that the extra moneys will have to come from the pockets of the book-buying public. It is a fact that most publishers could make a larger profit by closing down their businesses and simply investing the capital in stocks and shares or with a bank. Looking at the large profits reported by some of the publishing houses which are public companies, you may feel that there is no need to feel at all sorry for publishers and certainly no reason to believe that they could not afford to reward authors a little more generously. True, but the large, successful companies are very few in number, and you have to balance against them those which report losses and those which are forced to close down, and you have to realize that even in the best of times, many of the smaller companies, with fewer major authors to sustain them, find it very difficult to come out each year in the black.

What is needed for everyone's sake is a successful campaign to increase the sale of books, and the only way I can see of doing that (and forgive me for repeating it once more, but it is so important) is if the public can be convinced that books are value for money, and cheap at the price – which they undoubtedly are.

At the beginning of the MTA, you will have noticed that the proposed terms do not apply to books of which the illustrations are at least as important, if not more so, than the text, to technical books, manuals and reference books, textbooks written for the educational market, books involving three or more writers, and plays and poetry. It is unfortunately impossible here to advise authors on the terms which they should obtain for so many varieties of books which pose different problems and which are written and marketed in different ways from those of general books; but of course the main principles of the MTA should still apply. If in doubt about what is or is not an acceptable contract for such works, and if you do not have an agent, you can if you are a member seek advice from the Society of Authors or from the Writers' Guild.

Supposing that your publisher does not accept the MTA, and puts to you a contract which seems, to say the least, to be ungenerous, is there anything you can do? As I have mentioned earlier, unless you are a well-established author you have very little clout, but you can try a bit of gentle haggling. You will have to make your own judgement about how far the haggling can go, for if you press too hard the publisher may simply withdraw his offer and go to an author who will accept his terms without argument. But if he has gone as far as the preparation of a contract he is likely to be fairly deeply committed to your book, and he may have a little latitude on the terms. The publisher's position is often like that of someone attending an auction – he will have worked out in advance how much he can spend (or what terms he can offer on your book), but he will not necessarily bid the full amount at first. If the article being auctioned can be obtained (or your book signed up) for less than his planned maximum expenditure, he will have done well, but if he has to pay the full amount, he won't necessarily be very unhappy about it.

It is also worth remembering that contracts are not impossible to alter, even after you have signed them. If there is some point in the agreement over which you and your publisher do not see eye to eye, it may be possible to make an arrangement whereby the matter can be reviewed in, say, three years' time, and this is a course of action which is particularly advisable in such cases as when the publisher is asking to change from paying royalties on the published price to paying a percentage of his net receipts – you might decide to see how it works before committing yourself to it for ever.

Your problem with an agreement may not be concerned with terms so much as simply to understand what it means. Often the legal jargon is less than clear to the lay mind, and if, as sometimes happens, the publisher's form of agreement has been poorly drafted, it may not even make sense, or you may find that it contains two totally contradictory clauses. If you have no agent and are not a member of the Society of Authors or the Writers' Guild, what can you do? The first option open to you is simply to ask the publisher to explain everything that you do not understand. If you are still in doubt, another possible answer is to consult other authors, and if you do not know any, then you might consider joining your nearest Writers' Circle, which will almost certainly include among its members some published authors with experience of publisher's contracts. Or you can consult a solicitor, but with the greatest respect to the worthy firm which deals with the sale of your house, and the making of your Will, and other such everyday affairs, it is worth going to a firm which specializes in literary matters, for your family solicitor may well be as baffled as you by some of the technicalities of the business, and may cause irritation on all sides by quibbling over matters which truly are standard and acceptable practice in the book trade and missing the points that really should be queried. Of course, you may be lucky and have a family solicitor who already knows something about publisher's contracts, or who is clever enough to work it all out accurately for himself or diligent enough to find out from others what he does not know. The point is, of course, that you should only pay for advice if you are sure that it is going to be good and informed advice, and the cheapest way of making certain might be to join the Society of Authors or the Writers' Guild.

One last important point needs to be made. Much needed though a Minimum Terms Agreement has been, and just though its provisions are, there are many cases where an author should not feel guilty at accepting lesser terms. It is a matter for your personal judgement according to circumstances; your publisher may be particularly generous in certain respects and mean in others, and you may decide that the good more than makes up for the bad; or you may be aware that the market for your writing is so competitive that you are lucky to be published at all; or you may take the view that your publisher is so active on your behalf that it is better to receive a smaller royalty or share of subsidiary moneys from him than it would be to get better terms from another publisher who would sell far fewer copies or rights; or you might be content with a lower advance, knowing that it means that royalties are payable all the sooner. Those who have struggled to get the Minimum Terms Agreement accepted would undoubtedly say that every time you accept any terms which are worse than those laid down, you are letting down every other author and allowing the continued exploitation of authors. That is true. Authors should stick together, because it is the only way of improving their lot safely and permanently. Nevertheless, it is impossible to legislate for the circumstances surrounding the publication of every book and the relationship between every author and his publisher. You have to make your own reasonable judgement.

Author's Note

Since this book was written, regrettably little progress has been made. The Publishers Association has produced a Code of Practice in respect of authors' contracts, but its provisions do not go nearly as far as the Society of Authors and the Writers' Guild would wish, and in any case the Code is not binding on members of the Association. Negotiations (which still continue) between the Society and the Guild on the one hand and individual publishers on the other have resulted in the signing of a few Minimum Terms agreements, but the number is pitifully small. Apart from those two or three successes, all that can be said is that most publishers have become aware of the need to produce contracts which are more favourable to authors, and some have slightly improved their terms, but mostly in minor respects only.

It is important to note that in those MTAs which have been signed, the terms and the wording have not been exactly as shown on pages 93 to 104. The Society of Authors and the Writers' Guild have made certain concessions (meeting some of the objections mentioned on pages 105 to 123) and changes have been made to suit the special requirements of the publisher. The wording has also been altered in some clauses for the purposes of clarification. The basic principles, however, remain.

January, 1987.

6
Author/Publisher Relationships

Relationships between authors and publishers are often difficult, and have been so over a long period of time. The "Literature" section of *The Frank Muir Book* is full of anecdotes to illustrate this, and the list of authors who have written nastily about their publishers is lengthy and distinguished. Why there should be so much acrimony is hard to explain – not all publishers are ruthless exploiters of their authors – but I think it stems partly from the fact that very few authors understand much about publishing (which is why this book has been written), and even more from the other fact that, as a group, authors are trusting, not to say gullible.

It really is rather extraordinary. An author who would take the greatest care in the selection of any other person who is to perform some service for him, will happily place all his trust in a publisher of whom he knows nothing, and will expect him to behave with perfect efficiency, despite the fact that nothing else in this modern world, alas, can be relied upon to do so. We are all used to the trains that run late or are suddenly cancelled, to the garages which fail to cure the faults in our cars, to the builders who take longer than promised to complete their work and then charge more than their estimates. We grumble and pretend to be surprised when it happens, but we have been expecting the worst all along. Most authors, however, seem rarely to be prepared for any kind of inefficiency on the part of their publishers, and when inevitably it happens, they are not only shocked and angry, but usually very ready to believe that the publisher has done whatever it is deliberately, in a kind of personal attack. No wonder that the breaking point in the relationship can easily be reached.

The problem is always exacerbated by a failure to communicate – strange in a business so concerned with words – which is usually the publisher's fault. In all the years that I

dealt with authors I found them to be almost always understanding and co-operative when I took the time and trouble to
explain what was happening. But I didn't always manage it.
At one stage of my publishing career, when I joined a large
company as Editorial Director, I promised myself that I
would write regularly to all my authors to give them the latest
news on their books – where we had got to in production,
what luck we were having with subsidiary rights sales, and so
on. It never got done, alas, because there was just too much
pressure of other work. Don't be surprised, therefore, if there
are long periods of silence from your publisher. If the silence
goes on for too long, there is nothing to stop you writing with a
gentle reminder of your existence and a polite request for
information, but do try to avoid pestering. Do not, by the
way, try to interpret the silence of your publisher as being
significant or meaningful. No news is good news doesn't
necessarily apply – nor does the reverse. It may be just that
he's jolly busy.

Despite failures in communication, there is no reason why
publishers and authors should not be friends, especially since
they are both basically devoted to the same cause, providing
that, as in most human relationships, there is a certain amount
of give and take on both sides. The most difficult thing for an
author to understand is that his publisher is also concerned
with other books and other authors, and that his own book
may be one among, say, three hundred that the publisher is
working on during the year – it is one three-hundredth part of
his year; the most difficult thing for the publisher to remember is that the book represents many months or years of work
by the author, and that it is at the moment almost his entire
world.

If your publisher is not as friendly towards you as you would
like, behaving in an off-hand or superior way and making you
feel that you are wasting his time, then at the least he is
discourteous. But do remember that friendship is two-sided,
and make sure that you yourself are not the cause of his
attitude. If he likes your work, then he should be interested in
you as a person, and in your plans and your problems, but you
should equally be prepared to try to understand him and his
difficulties, and to enter your relationship with him in neither
too aggressive nor too defensive an attitude. If he seems to
brush aside some of the things that worry you, be aware that
in his eyes almost all authors have the same kind of problems:

they are almost always all discontented with their sales, disappointed that their books have not been advertised, feel that their publishers are not making sufficient effort for them; they all get afflicted from time to time with writer's block (when the new book has got stuck, and the author despairs of making progress with it); they are all short of money (who isn't? But authors seem to live from hand to mouth, and that applies to bestselling writers too, many of whom are up to their eyes in debt to the Inland Revenue and have ex-wives to support and an expensive life-style which they refuse to abandon); and they all believe the grass is greener on the other side of the fence. The publisher has heard the same stories before and will hear them many times again; if he is a good friend, he will try not to let that show, but if he does, do try to understand, and realize too that it may not only be other authors and books which make him seem preoccupied, but also the problems of finance and administration and all the other troubles of business life which may be on his mind.

There may be more than a slight lack of friendliness in the relationship, and you may, for instance, suspect that your publisher is deliberately avoiding you if every time you phone him you are told, "I'm sorry, he's in a meeting." Of course, it may be true. Publishing used to be an autocratic business with decisions taken by the head of the house or by those individuals to whom he had delegated authority; nowadays, it is a question of management by committee. Your publisher may indeed be in a meeting, to discuss editorial matters, or jackets, or publicity and promotion, or sales plans, or budgets and five-year plans, or staff salaries – not to mention the possibility that he may be talking to another author on his list.

On the other hand he may indeed be trying to avoid speaking to you. Why? Possibly because he has not yet come to a decision about your book, or is having difficulty in persuading others in the firm to share his enthusiasm for it, and is reluctant to tell you yet again that you have to be patient. Or perhaps he has decided to reject your book, and being a coward, prefers to tell you so by letter rather than on the phone. Or perhaps he has forgotten until your name is mentioned that he promised to look into some matter, and not having done so, is unwilling to expose his failing. All very unsatisfactory from your point of view, but also very human, and perhaps if you try very hard you can find enough of the divine in yourself to forgive.

However, if you are constantly told that he is in a meeting, and if additionally he never rings back as promised, and fails to answer your letters, and in general takes considerable pains to avoid any contact with you, then either he is a rotten publisher (and probably has a rotten secretary into the bargain), or perhaps you are a Difficult Author. Difficult Authors are those who, among other unpleasant habits, phone daily (usually to say that their book is unavailable in such-and-such a bookshop), expect to be received immediately if they call unannounced at the publisher's offices, ask their publishers to undertake any of their research which they find too difficult, believe that it is their publisher's responsibility to make their hotel and theatre bookings, instruct the publisher to obtain books for them from other publishers at trade discount, rewrite their books at proof stage, demand that the part of the advance due on publication should be paid now, although the book is not even half way to completion, and, above all, argue over everything from a changed comma to the date chosen for publication, and who constantly complain. If you are that sort of author (and, believe me, there are plenty of them around), be prepared for your publisher not only to be permanently in a meeting, but also to reject your next book, since he may well have decided that life is too short to make it worth putting up with you.

"I recognize myself as a Difficult Author," you may bravely say, "at least in part. But the reason that I argue and complain constantly is simply that he is both rude and extremely inefficient." Well, maybe you're right. I just hope that you tried being reasonable first. In all walks of life, some people find it easy to be aggrieved, and if you are one of them, then however justified your complaints may be, your attitude may only succeed in antagonizing the one person who might be able to put right whatever is wrong, and increasing harassment on your part may simply lead to greater inefficiency on his.

On the other hand, there are of course times when authors should complain, and forcefully too. Publishers are undoubtedly often incompetent, and when they make stupid mistakes or fall down on promises, you are entitled to be angry. Why should publishers so often be inefficient? There are, I think, several factors to be considered. First of all, there is the fact that every book is different, with its own peculiarities and problems, and there is no universal formula which can be applied to the solution of its individual difficulties; this clearly multiplies the opportunities for human error. Secondly, publishing is a comparatively complex business, involving in all its processes not only a large number of people and many skills, but also quite a few sub-contractors, who are not totally subject to the publisher's control; this again makes publishing particularly vulnerable to Sod's Law ("if anything can go wrong, it will"). Thirdly, the expansion of the trade has led to additional inefficiency – and this point needs more detailed explanation.

For many reasons, publishers' output has increased dramatically compared with the numbers of books published, for example, between the two World Wars. It is partly due to the "explosion" in reading which took place during the Second World War, the higher educational standards now existing, which mean that more of the population can read, and the techniques of production and marketing which have made books not only readily available but, in the case of paperbacks, much more acceptable to the general public than they were (many people still find a bookshop a somewhat forbidding place and would not think of going into one, whereas there is nothing frightening about the paperbacks in the newsagent's racks). But economic factors have also played a major role in increasing the numbers of books published. Many years ago, sweated labour in the printing and binding trades and low-paid but dedicated workers in publishers' offices made it possible to make a profit with small numbers of books, especially at a time when Britannia not only ruled the waves, which was important in terms of overseas markets, but also sat firmly on inflation; nowadays, however, workers in most industries are reasonably paid, inflation goes on galloping upwards, and book prices have never rocketed sufficiently to keep pace with the financial pressures imposed on the business by the outside world. Now, when you can no longer make a large profit on a successful book, and your safety nets on an unsuccessful book (by which I mean your ability to part-produce a very small quantity and your facilities for disposing of your overstocks by reducing the retail price and still making a profit) have disappeared, then your readiest answer to the problem is to publish more. (And this is when, incidentally, books turn into "product", which term inevitably means a diminution of the human relationship which should count for so much in the publication of a book.) You may make less profit on each title, but you will hope that greater volume will maintain your firm's overall results. This very often leads in turn to the rule of the accountants, of which I have already written, which is not always the most efficient way to run the business, and it will also mean an increase in staff. Now, despite better education for all, the general standard of work produced by junior staff in offices these days is very much lower than it used to be before the Second World War. People often seem more concerned about job definitions and whether or not they get luncheon vouchers, than with the quality of their work. They don't *care*. And those who do care, especially in the higher ranks, are frequently so overburdened that to their despair they cannot give the attention to detail that they would like. This is where the inefficiency comes from, this is why computers are fed with inaccurate information, this is where muddle is swept under the carpet – and this is where, if the sack is threatened, the union will step in to protect the employee. And of course it is all a situation which lends itself admirably to the application of the Peter Principle of eventual promotion beyond the level of the employee's capability.

Whatever the cause of publisher's incompetence, if you encounter it you should certainly complain. But do make sure, before you do, that it really is incompetence and that it really is the publisher's fault – the absence of your book from bookshops, for instance, to take a very common cause of complaint, may not be due to the publisher's failings, whatever the bookseller says. It is worth listening to both sides of the story, so try to present your grievances in a reasoned and reasonable manner, and listen to what your publisher has to say in his defence, and be prepared to apologize if you are wrong. You are fully entitled to a hearing and courtesy from him, and he is entitled to the same from you. Incidentally, if you receive no satisfaction from your contact in the publisher's office, there is nothing to stop you going over his head (assuming that he has a superior), but again make sure that your complaint is justified.

In his biography of the founder of Penguin Books, *Allen Lane: King Penguin*, Jack Morpurgo wrote:

> Publishers are convinced that most authors are ignorant of the techniques of the publishing craft and suspect, often with justification, that many sustain this ignorance by a lofty conviction that comprehending the technical and commercial practicalities

of publishing is somehow beneath their dignity and an unnecessary distraction from their prime duty, to set words, ideas or narrative to paper. Understanding the means whereby their handsomely embellished paper is to be reproduced, promoted, distributed and made profitable – to both publisher and author – is a process to which they need only give such thought as is, in their opinion, unavoidable."

Pretty harsh, you may think, but the point is that our world has increasingly become one for professionals, and even if you are no more than a part-time writer, you need to be professional in your approach, which means, among other things, learning about writing and learning something about publishing.

You also need to be professional in your approach if you become involved in a serious dispute with your publisher. Seek expert advice at an early stage and give your adviser as fair an account of what has happened as you can manage, trying not to conceal from him anything which may be to your disadvantage – he will give better advice if he knows the whole story. When you have taken advice, or even if you have not, try to write to the publisher in moderate terms – nothing is ever achieved by abuse. If you have correspondence with an adviser, do not show it to the publisher. Think before taking any too hasty action.

So far in this chapter, I have referred to the author/publisher relationship, but in most cases it is more likely to be specifically an editor with whom the author has contact. A publisher's editor is not merely someone who purchases books from authors and then passes them on to be turned into printed and bound books. He is in most cases truly an editor, in the sense that he becomes involved with the actual writing of the book, perhaps as a critic who asks the author to make changes, perhaps even altering the book himself. Not many authors manage to produce a perfect book, and a good partnership between author and editor will often result in a worthwhile improvement.

Few authors are capable of viewing their own books dispassionately, and even wives or husbands, whom so many writers credit in their acknowledgements as being their most severe critics, are often themselves too close to the work in question to see it plainly. A good editor is distant enough to see the book clearly and will tell the author what, if anything, he thinks is wrong with it, but at the same time is sufficiently in tune with the author's intentions to do so sympathetically. During the whole of my publishing career, I followed the principle that in such matters the author's decision would be final – it was his book, not mine, and if he disagreed with me, then, unless my criticisms were so fundamental that I felt I could not publish the book unless he made the changes I wanted, I would give way to him. But this bargain on my part was contingent on the author's willingness to listen most carefully to my comments, to discuss them with me, and to be prepared to admit that I might possibly occasionally be right. I tried always to make it clear to the author that I was not interested in making alterations simply to justify my own existence or to boost my ego so that I could boast afterwards that the book was partly my work, but simply to make it a better book. Any sensible author will, I think, welcome such an approach, but there are some who find an editor's suggestions an intolerable interference, however gently the criticisms are made, and believe me, such is the sensitivity of some authors that editors often have to be extremely careful not to offend or discourage.

Of course, some editors adopt a much more dictatorial approach, and many authors complain of their arrogance. It is very difficult to deal with this kind of high-handedness, especially when it comes from someone covering up his own uncertainties with an aggressive insistence on being right. Unless you can swallow this, your only course is to go over the editor's head to his director, in the hope of getting a more sympathetic hearing. If that fails, or is impossible because the arrogant editor is himself the highest authority in the firm, then you have to choose between withdrawing your book and repaying any moneys you have received on account of it, or of letting it go through in a form which you dislike, and to do that will probably sour your whole relationship with the company and make you dissatisfied with every aspect of the publication. There is not a great deal to be gained in having an ongoing angry relationship with your publisher, and it is much better to make a clean break. But of course it is easy to say that, and not necessarily easy to find another home for the book. And that thought brings me back to the plea that you should listen carefully to the publisher's comments, and discuss them without heat, and accept his wishes if you can bring yourself to do so. Even arrogant editors are right sometimes.

If you stay with your publisher despite the disagreements, it may be possible to save yourself some of the trouble on your next book by discussing the project in much greater detail with your editor before you begin to write.

American editors tend to be far more insistent on working on an author's typescript than most of their British counterparts, and some authors find their editing very disturbing. It is difficult to know what to advise without going into specific cases, but in general the usual rules apply: plead your case as strongly as you can, having first considered seriously whether the editor might possibly be right, and if you get nowhere, then decide whether you want to stand on your dignity and cancel the contract, or whether you will cry about the alterations all the way to the bank.

It is worth repeating that an editor's intentions are always to improve the book, but that he does have more than one duty. An author once asked me whose interests came first with me – his, or my own and those of my firm. It's a difficult question to answer in black and white terms. Publishers understand very well that they are middlemen, dependent for their livelihood on authors, and in general they try to be sympathetic to writers and their work and problems. But if there is a conflict between their duty to an individual author and to themselves and their firm, they will naturally opt for the latter, and it would be foolish to pretend otherwise. We are all selfish to some degree or other.

Of course, no alterations of any kind should be made to a book without the author's consent. Should you find at proof stage that your book has been altered, and that is the first you know of it, you are entitled to object most strongly. Even if the book is the better for the alterations, you can accept the changes with gratitude, but still protest firmly that you should have been consulted. There is a vital principle here – that the author's work must not be altered without his permission. Most good publishers respect that rule, though they may feel it should not be necessary to check with the author such minor changes as the correction of typing errors, spelling and punctuation, or alterations made to bring the typescript into line with the publisher's house style (which is usually concerned with questions like the use of capital letters, whether quotation marks should be double or single, consistency in layout and the numbering of sub-paragraphs, and so on). They may also correct obvious mistakes which appear to be unintentional on the author's part and which are probably due simply to a lapse of memory. But any of the minor alterations mentioned can infuriate the author rather than please him, and it is my belief that the publisher should discuss the matter with the author before he begins any copy-editing work on the type-script, and should come to some agreement about the extent to which the author feels he should be consulted about changes. If your publisher does not raise the matter with you, ask him about it.

A question that arises frequently is the stage at which an author and an editor should work together on a book. If you have sent in a completed typescript, there is obviously no problem, but if you are an established author on the list or are lucky enough to have been commissioned, it is a very good idea to discuss the book as fully as possible with the editor before you begin to write, and perhaps to show him the early pages as you produce them. Some authors hate to talk about their books in advance, and cannot bear to let anyone read a word of the book until it is finished, but if you can let your editor see the first few chapters, it may save a lot of grief at a later stage, because he may be able to point out where, if at all, you are going wrong, or how you might improve the book. He may also of course tell you things which irritate because you are already aware of them and intend to do something about them at a later stage in the writing, but you will simply have to put up with that. One thing to try to avoid is sending your book in chapter by chapter for criticism; since your editor will have read dozens of books between your sending in one chapter and the next, he will probably have to refresh his memory by re-reading the first chapter when the second comes in, and so on, which he may well find extremely time-consuming and boring. If you are going to show your work in parts, send a good chunk at a time.

If you want him to be, your editor will probably be willing to be adviser, sounding-board, critic, comforter, shoulder-to-weep-on, inspirer and friend, despite the fact that the most kind-hearted, considerate, undemanding human beings do sometimes undergo a transformation when they become au-thors – not necessarily in their everyday lives, but in anything which concerns their book – turning into egotistical, thought-less, ruthless monsters – often pleasant monsters for most of the time, but monsters nevertheless. If you become friendly with your editor, beware – and the closer the relationship is the more there is need to take care – that you do not impose on him. He does have a life of his own to lead, and when he is out of the office may be very glad to get away from books (even yours) for a while. So phone him at the office rather than in his home if you want to talk business. And he will appreciate a word of thanks now and then.

It always seems to me a pity when authors who live a long way away from their publishers never get to meet their editors. A face-to-face encounter is so much more helpful in establishing a relationship than any amount of telephone calls and letters. The cost of travel is such that it may be prohibitive for some authors to visit their publisher even once (though of course the expense can be claimed against tax), but if you have any opportunity to visit the city or town where your publisher works, do make a point of calling to see him, writing first to make an appointment.

How do certain editors get involved with this or that book and its author? The process is often somewhat haphazard for new authors. If the book is clearly of considerable import-ance, the editor who works on it will almost certainly be one of some seniority and experience. In a general publishing house most editors have certain special interests, so if your book falls into a specialist category, it will go to the editor responsible for that part of the list. Other books or authors may have been "discovered" by an editor, who will probably continue to deal with the books concerned.

Many books may be allocated to an editor much more arbitrarily: "This looks like an easy one – you'd better take it, Miss Junior"; or, "Who wants to read this book on Prostitu-tion in Edwardian London? It looks as though it's very popular in approach, so we won't send it out for an expert reading until we've looked at it in house. Who wants it? No one? Then you'd better glance at it, Mr Senior – you've got less of a load this week than the rest of us." Naturally, this kind of process results sometimes in books being handled by rather unsuitable editors, but the editorial director of the firm will usually keep an eye on things and give the book to someone else if it is obvious that the original editor cannot cope.

Can an editor judge a book which is not to his personal taste or on a subject in which he is not expert? The answer is that good editors can at least recognize the merits or failings of such a book. They cannot always eliminate their personal feelings, but they try to be representative of the average reader and to judge by the standards of the genre. So you may well find someone whose literary idols are of the calibre of, say, Proust working happily and successfully as an editor of pulp fiction (well, perhaps that is an exaggeration, though the principle holds good). As for expertise, as I have said elsewhere, most publishers use expert outside readers to check the accuracy and validity of specialist books, but the experienced editor will at least be able to judge something of the quality of the book and its likely appeal to the public. He may also, in the course of working on a number of such books, have become, if not an expert, at least very knowledgeable on the subject himself.

Should you stay with the same publisher all the time? It may be of course that you are prolific and/or versatile, in which case you may need more than one publisher. Too many new books by one author appearing on the same publisher's list can, unless you are particularly well known, sometimes hamper each other's sales. Such authors sometimes use pseudonyms and often have a number of publishers. In the same way, if you write on a variety of subjects, you may need to be published by different houses specializing in your different kinds of book. It will be as well to keep your first publisher ("Publisher A") informed of your other plans, and indeed you may wish to make it clear that he will continue to have first offer of all your books in the genre with which he first began to publish you, whereas your books of a different kind will be offered to Publisher B, and a third variety to Publisher C. If A, B and C all know where they stand in relation to you and your work, there should be no cause for dissension.

For the average author, however, unless you are very dissatisfied with your publisher, and if he wants to go on publishing your books and you continue to write the kind of thing which is suited to his list, then undoubtedly you should stay with him. Publishers sometimes feel that some authors show far too little loyalty. The publisher may have brought out the first few books by an author, including perhaps work which was not of his finest, gradually building up his reputation, and then the writer produces an important book which finally establishes his success and goes off to another publisher who reaps the benefit of the first publisher's work and faith. Usually, the author is wooed and flattered by the second publisher, who offers him not only a larger advance than he has been used to getting, but promises him more promotion and publicity, full consultation, etc, etc. Beware of such offers. Many an author has moved to a different firm only to find that he is really no better off than he was before. On the other hand, if for some reason you are unhappy with your present publisher and you get an offer from elsewhere, of course it is right to move, but I think it is fair first to discuss the matter with your present publisher, presenting him frankly with your reasons for discontent and offering him the opportunity of putting right whatever it is that is wrong. If he cannot do so, then he will probably not resist your parting too strongly, for no good publisher can work to the best advantage with an author who is unhappy on his list. But again, you may find that you have jumped from the frying pan into the fire.

Of course it is much more shattering when it happens the other way round, as it were. Here you are, having had half a dozen books published by the same house, and suddenly they turn round and say that they do not want to go ahead with your new book, which they may even admit is just as good as its predecessors. The only explanation you will probably get is that the market for your kind of book has declined to a point where it is no longer economical to publish your work. Sorry, and all that. Your only hope then is to find another publisher who has perhaps a more vigorous sales approach, or lower overheads, or some other quality or set of circumstances which will allow him to go on bringing out your kind of book. It is not a very hopeful outlook. Your other alternative is to write a better book. Easier said than done, of course, but maybe if you change to a different genre you might do better. Study the market too. One of the reasons that the publisher has declined your new book may simply be that it is of a kind that has gone somewhat out of fashion. All writers should read voraciously, partly to study how other authors achieve their effects and to learn from them, but partly, including new books in their diet, to see what the latest trends are. I would also like to suggest that you should read widely. Naturally, you will choose principally the kind of writing which interests you most, but if you read nothing but biography, or poetry, or fiction, or travel, or whatever it may be, you are missing a great deal. And I find it astonishing that many authors will boast that they never read the work of other writers in their own field. That seems an ostrich-like attitude.

In speaking of author/publisher relationships, I have emphasized the role of the editor. He is likely to be the person in your publishing house with whom you deal most of the time, but it is as well to meet others who will be working on your book if you can – among them I would single out the sales director, whoever is in charge of publicity and promotion, the production manager, the person who prepares the royalty statements, and the subsidiary rights manager. It does no harm either to make contact with the managing director. Indeed, the more people in your publishing house that you know, the better, and you should feel free to contact any of them direct if you have a query or complaint which falls within their sphere. Since, however, your editor is your prime colleague, it is worth making a point of keeping him informed about any dealings you may have with other members of the staff. It saves the wires from getting crossed.

All of us who write dream from time to time if not of great financial rewards from our writing, then at least of gaining the kind of recognition and respect for our work which will mean that we never again have trouble in finding a publisher and that the firm concerned will give us first-class attention at all times. (If we were in that position, we should probably have the great financial rewards too!) Well, we can dream. But being realistic, admitting that we are not in the great best-seller class or recognized as one of the twentieth century's greater geniuses, we should plant our feet firmly on the earth. No sensible author turns to writing full time unless he is assured of being able to support himself and his family, probably with an income from another source. No sensible author builds his hopes too high, nor expects everything he writes to reach the same level of success. No sensible author forgets that it is not only the quality of his work which determines how well his book does, but remembers that there are other factors, such as fashion, booms and recessions, and luck. No sensible author neglects to understand that his relationship with his publisher, however friendly it may be, is basically a business one, liable to change, or that his publisher and the rest of the staff are human and liable to make mistakes. No sensible author believes that everyone is perfect – even himself.

7
Reasons for Complaint

The publisher has lost my material

Given the fact that several hundred typescripts flow in and out of most publishers' offices every year, it is surprising perhaps that they do not get lost more often, especially since publishing tends to be a rather untidy business. If your publisher has lost your typescript, not too much harm will have been done, though it may be very inconvenient, provided you still have a copy; if he has any sense of responsibility he will pay for the typescript to be replaced or at least contribute part of the cost, despite the fact that his form letter or card acknowledging receipt of your book in his offices probably states somewhere that he will accept no liability for the loss or damage of your material while it is in his possession. The loss or damage of other materials, such as illustrations, transparencies, or perhaps goods of some value which are to be photographed in order to illustrate the book, is a much more serious matter, since they may be extremely costly or impossible to replace. The only solution is to take out an insurance against loss or damage. Your publisher may be prepared to pay the premium himself, but it is more likely that at best he will agree to share it. The rights and wrongs of the matter are hard to define, depending on circumstances in each case, but broadly speaking, if you are sending the material to the publisher unsolicited, the responsibility for insuring valuables is yours, but if he has asked for them, he should, in my view, be prepared at least to share in the cost. It is important that he should understand what sum could be considered reasonable compensation for loss or damage, and you should leave him in no doubt about that. The Institute of Photographers can give advice on the appropriate amounts.

My book has been rejected for political reasons

If you write a book which takes a political position, or attacks or defends certain views, the book may be rejected solely because of the contents rather than because of any lack of quality. Some naïve authors believe that publishers have no right to turn down such a book and that it is their duty to publish any book which is adequately written and saleable. Not true. Publishers still, fortunately, have freedom of personal choice. If you receive such a rejection it suggests that you have not done your market research. Choose another publisher whose existing list demonstrates that he will be sympathetic to your views.

I put up an idea to a publisher who rejected it and then immediately commissioned another author to write a book on the very same subject

This is very unfortunate, especially since ideas are not protected by copyright, and in any case it would be difficult to prove that the publisher has in fact pinched the one you suggested to him. The use of someone's idea without his permission is certainly unethical and most reputable publishers would try to avoid doing anything of the kind, but editors cannot always control their subconscious minds and may use your idea without any intention of stealing it, believing that it is original to themselves. "A likely story," you may say, but I can only repeat that good publishers do not do naughty things deliberately. Active editors conceive a large number of books, and get their inspiration from hundreds of different sources. Very occasionally, recognizing that a concept stems from a book they have rejected, they may even suggest that you should have some payment for the idea though they want someone else to write the book. You may not like that either, but it is difficult to know what to do about it.

My hardcover publisher also controls a paperback company and other concerns which utilize other subsidiary rights. He wants me to give him all those rights, though I would prefer to let the competition have an opportunity to bid for them

Many authors would think you lucky to have this automatic interest in the subsidiary rights of your book. If you are really unhappy about it, you should take your book elsewhere – there are still many publishers who do not have any direct links with the users of subsidiary rights. In today's difficult conditions, however, you should probably accept the offer with gratitude, though you might try asking the publisher whether he would accept a "topping right" arrangement, which would mean that he had to submit the subsidiary rights to other concerns but would have the right to buy them himself by topping, or improving on, the best bids he received.

My publisher wants to break my contract

The fundamental points in a publishing contract are that the author has written or agrees to write a book and the publisher undertakes to publish it. There are many side issues which may give rise to breach of contract by either party, but they are insignificant in comparison with a decision by the publisher not to proceed with the publication of the author's book.

The publisher may have many possible reasons for such a decision. Sometimes it results from recognizable failings on the part of the author: perhaps the completed work differs substantially from the synopsis on which it was commissioned, or is much shorter or longer than the extent specified in the contract, or the author has been so tardy in delivering it that the market for it no longer exists, or because the book is clearly libellous. All is not necessarily lost in such situations, since the author may be able to avert disaster by doing extra work on the book. If he refuses to do so, or is incapable of making the necessary alterations, he cannot be too indignant when the publisher wants to cancel the contract.

The agreement may be rather more arbitrarily rescinded on the basis of failings on the author's part, either real or imaginary, if there is an "acceptance" clause in the contract (see p. 107), and it is often very difficult to argue in such cases since the publisher's personal taste and views are involved.

Contracts are sometimes broken because the editor who bought the book has left the firm, and there is no longer anyone working there to care about the book. Everyone in a publishing firm should care about all the books on the list, of course, but in practice many books get published because a single person in the publishing concern is enthusiastic about them, and if that person leaves, those who take over his work may be indifferent or even hostile to those books. "I always thought we were crazy to buy that," the new editor may say. "We only took it on because So-and-so was so enthusiastic about it." To find not only that your friendly editor has left the firm, but that as a result your publishing contract is about to be cancelled, will be a terrible blow, but a book published without any enthusiasm will do little good for anyone concerned. Of course, this kind of thing does not happen with all the books on the list of an editor who leaves his firm, many of which will have wide support from the rest of the staff, and it tends to occur with books which would be borderline prospects in any publishing house. In the United States editors seem to move regularly from one publishing concern to another, but they frequently take their authors with them, so this question does not arise to the same extent.

The major problem nowadays is that cancellations made because the publisher is reducing his output have become a commonplace. There is nothing wrong with the typescript, but the publisher decides that he will lose less by cutting the book from his list than by proceeding with it. Any book which does not show a high profit margin is a candidate for the axe, even though the author has been published successfully by that house for many years, and in some cases the entire list has disappeared as the publisher has gone out of business.

What is the author's course of action when it happens? The first thing is to ask whether anything can be done to alter the publisher's decision, such as cutting the book to make it more economic, or making changes designed to widen its appeal. The publisher's reply is likely to be a firm rejection of all recipes for salvaging the book, since he has probably already considered all such possibilities and decided that nothing will solve his basic problem, which is that he just won't sell sufficient copies.

You are now left with two alternatives. The first is to insist, possibly with the threat of legal action, that the publisher comply with the terms of the contract and that he publish the book despite his wish not to do so. In general, this is not a course to be recommended. It may be extremely difficult if not impossible to force him to publish, and even if you succeed in so doing, he will almost certainly print a minimum quantity of the book and make only sufficient effort at selling it to recoup his costs. Your relationship with him is bound to be a bitter one, and few authors who force their publishers to bring out a book can really rejoice in the results.

The second alternative is to be compensated by the publisher. Some publishers will try to persuade you that their liability should be limited to any part of the advance already paid, but this is hardly fair, and you should ask for at least the balance of the advance and preferably a total sum (including any advance already paid) equal to the amount that the book might have been expected to earn for you. Each case is different, and it is impossible to lay down any hard and fast rules about the amount of compensatory payments which is fair, but if you have no agent, you should seek professional advice, either from the Society of Authors or the Writers' Guild, if you are a member, or from a good solicitor.

In any case, as well as compensation, or even if the fault lies with you and you are not entitled to any money, you should obtain from the defaulting publisher an official letter confirming that all rights in the book in question have reverted to you and that the publisher has no further claim on you whatsoever. You should also ensure that all material supplied by you to the publisher is returned. You are then free to place the book with another house if you can. Some publishers, when paying compensation, ask that the sums paid shall be returned by the author if he places the book elsewhere, arguing that he should not be paid twice for the same work. Circumstances vary, of course, and there may be some cases where it would be reasonable to agree to return part of the compensation money if you sell the book to another publisher, but in general you should never return the whole amount – at the very least, the rejection will have lost you time and caused you considerable anguish, for both of which you deserve compensation. The publisher may argue that he has already lost money on the book and that you should be prepared to share in the loss. "You have had part of the advance, and you have got all the rights back – surely that should be sufficient." It is a time to be tough. You are more likely to suffer from the non-publication than he is, and in any case he is quite likely to have already calculated the cancellation in terms of paying you a full compensation, and is now simply trying to save his firm a little money. You can't blame him for that, but you don't have to accept the terms he first offers without trying to better the deal from your point of view.

In extreme cases – if, for instance, the firm is already bankrupt – you may not get any compensation, though you should still make a claim, and also be sure that you get your rights back. However sympathetic you feel towards the publisher in his dire straits and the members of his staff who are now without jobs, you have to put your own interests first.

At the same time, a plea for consideration. It costs nothing for you to start off with a conciliatory attitude. Remember that the person giving you the bad news is unlikely to be enjoying the situation, which has not been devised simply to annoy you; the easier you make it for him, the easier in the end it may be for you to negotiate a settlement to your satisfaction. Litigation is to be avoided if possible.

One other circumstance might be mentioned: the occasion when your publisher declines to publish your book on the grounds that it "will do your reputation no good", but, on the assumption that it will be up to your usual standard, wishes to publish your next book. To put the book on one side may mean that you have lost the work of a year or more, and you have the choice of listening to what he says and allowing yourself to be convinced, or of parting company with him and taking the book to another publisher. Before you choose the latter course, you will have to decide whether or not your relationship with your present publisher is worth preserving, despite the disappointment he has just handed you, and that may depend not only on the way he has treated you in the past, but also on whether you believe he could possibly be right about this book. It would be in order to ask to see the reports on it, and, if you are not fully convinced, perhaps to ask that the book should be sent to another reader, without comment from the publisher and perhaps without your name on the typescript, in order to get one more independent judgement, though of course such a report would have to be very favourable to outweigh the previous adverse comments. If you already have a contract for the book, and it is decided that the publisher will not go ahead, you are back in the situation described above when some sort of compensation is in order. Just be sure that your own assessment of the work is right, and his wrong, before you finally burn your boats.

My publisher wants to reduce my royalties

As an alternative to cancelling the contract, some publishers ask authors to take a lower royalty or a smaller share of subsidiary rights than those specified in the contract. The author in this situation is facing a nasty dilemma: if he refuses to accept the lower rates, the publisher may cancel the contract altogether; if he accepts them, he is not only going to make less money than he should, but may also be setting an unhappy precedent, not only for himself, but for other authors too. Publishers are often quite adept at using the ploy, "Mr Scribble and Ms Copperplate have already agreed to similar terms," to make you feel that you are being unreasonable if you demur.

I should make it clear that I am not referring to the clause in many agreements which says that the royalty payable on "small reprints shall be at the minimum rate". In that case, the publisher is only asking to revert to the royalty rate payable on the first sales of the book, even though sales have reached the level when higher rates come into force. No, I am talking here of what amounts to a re-negotiation of all the financial terms of the contract, so that, for instance, the basic starting royalty rate of 10% is to be reduced to 7½%.

The only answer is to find out all you can about the circumstances, including if possible details of the publisher's costing and expected profit, and then to make a judgement. If you insist on a full royalty, will he really either cancel the book or lose sales because its retail price will be too high? And supposing you agree to reduce your earnings, can you be sure that he is also suffering to some extent? Are you in a buyer's or a seller's market? When you have considered all the factors, you can make your mind up. If you decide to accept lower rates, at least make sure that you have it in writing that your agreement is not to be taken as a precedent.

My editor has left and I don't know anyone at my publisher's now

Even if, supposing that your editor leaves your publisher, there is no question of cancelling your contract, you may be faced with the lesser but nevertheless worrying problem of not knowing who will be dealing with your book in future. When an editor, or any other member of the staff, leaves, his work is naturally passed over to a successor, or sometimes shared out between a number of people. Whoever has taken over responsibility for you and your book should write and introduce himself, and perhaps suggest a meeting so that you can get to know each other. Sometimes, however, it is not done – perhaps because, with the best of intentions, your new contact finds himself so overburdened with his new responsibilities that he just doesn't get around to writing to you, or perhaps because publishers are human and, as with any other group of men and women, include some who are lazy or inefficient or discourteous, or all three.

If after a while you have heard nothing except that your former editor has departed, write to the head of the department, if there is one, or to a director of the company, and ask to be put in touch with your new editor. You shouldn't have to do this, but it is better than just sitting at home waiting for a word which may never come. Then, when you have written or spoken on the phone, if your new editor makes no suggestions of a meeting, propose it yourself.

It may happen that when you meet your new editor, you do not get on with him – and we all meet people from time to time to whom we are not sympathetic. In this case I suggest that you write a tactful letter to his superior in the publishing house, asking if there is anyone else that you could deal with. If you make it clear that you accept that there may be faults on both sides, no one's feelings will be badly hurt, and a change may be possible. Of course, your new contact may now be the only editor in the firm, or perhaps is the Managing Director himself. Your only solution then is either to grin and bear it or to find another publisher.

My publisher has made editorial changes to my book

Publishers regularly make changes in authors' typescripts before they are sent to the printer. Since extraordinarily large numbers of authors cannot spell, know little about punctuation, are frequently inconsistent and often inaccurate, the service that publishers provide in these respects is something to be grateful for. If you happen to be meticulous in such matters and indeed feel strongly about your commas and full stops, or if you are deliberately using a particular kind of spelling for effect, or indeed are departing from the normal rules in any way, it is as well to discuss the matter at an early stage with your editor, and to put a note at the front of the typescript, addressed to both copy editor and printer, asking them to respect your intentions and not to alter your work.

In any case, unless the publisher's alterations are of the most minor kind and you have already given blanket permission for them to be made, you should be given the opportunity of seeing and approving the changes before the typescript goes to the printer. If alterations have been made of which you strongly disapprove, particularly if the emphasis or spirit of the writing has been changed, you would be within your rights to insist on the reinstatement of your original version, even at proof stage. Nothing should be done to your typescript without your consent. But at the same time do be reasonable, listen to the copy editor's justification of what has been done, and if the changes improve the book, be ready to acknowledge the fact and perhaps even to thank the person who carried them out.

I get no editorial help

It has long been said that British editors are over-reluctant to help their authors to improve their books (or perhaps incapable of doing so), whereas American editors go to the other extreme and often virtually rewrite books which had no need of such treatment. If your editor does not help you, it may be simply that he doesn't see anything wrong with the book (in which case it is either perfect as it stands, or more likely he is a less than perfect editor), or that he knows that something is wrong, but cannot really put his finger on what it is, or cannot clarify the problem sufficiently for you to understand it too; or it may be that he expects you, as the author, to have a more dispassionate view of your work than in fact you have, so that if he says, for instance, that it needs a bit of cutting, or that such and such a part needs strengthening, you will understand what he means without him needing to spell it out. Most authors find it very difficult to view their work from sufficient distance, but some editors find that hard to understand. If that is the problem, you can try asking him to explain in much greater detail. If he cannot do so, then once again you are faced with a less than perfect editor, and your only course is probably to change publishers if you can.

Of course, one other possible reason why you do not get editorial help is that you have demonstrated in the past that you really don't want it. With some of their authors, editors have to tread extremely delicately, knowing that the least hint of criticism will be greeted with anger, abuse, hysterics, the sulks, argument, or at very least will be totally ignored, despite the fact that the author begged for comments and advice. Criticism hurts, but it should always be listened to.

The title of my book has been changed without my approval

Everyone agrees that a good title is extremely important, and the only problem is to decide what constitutes a good one. We can all recognize them after the event, but not always before-hand. The story has often been told of that great publisher Stanley Unwin consulting booksellers about a book which he was going to publish and which had already earned itself some reputation. Many advised him to change the title, saying that "expedition" was an old-fashioned word to use for a true adventure story, and that no one would be able to remember or pronounce the second word of the title. He refused to change it. The book was of course *The Kon-Tiki Expedition*.

As a general principle, it should go without saying that a title should not be changed without the author's approval, but in this business the old adage that two heads are better than one is very often true, and if a publisher wants to change a book's title, and is prepared to explain sensibly his reasons for doing so, the author should be prepared to be convinced. If he is not, he may be able to force his publisher to use his original title, but no one is going to be very happy about it.

My proof corrections have not been followed

When your publisher sends you proofs to correct and you mark them up, using all the standard signs, making sure that all your corrections are totally unambiguous, it is very dis-appointing to find sometimes that in the finished book the corrections have not been made, or that new errors have occurred. By all means protest to your publisher if this happens, but unless the errors are of a very serious nature, it is unlikely that he will be able to do anything about it, at least until he reprints the book (if he does). Why are corrections ignored, and why do new errors appear? Usually as a result of carelessness at the printers. There is little you can do, except to hope that your publisher will use one of the better printers next time, and that the printer's staff will be among those who still take a pride in the quality of their work.

In times gone by, most printers demanded a very high standard from their compositors, and literal errors were rare; moreover, printers employed expert and often very erudite readers who would mark corrections and queries on the proofs before they were sent out to the author. Nowadays, alas, standards are much lower, and often the proofs are not read by the printer at all.

Another cause of complaint is when printing errors are not corrected in a reprint, despite the fact that the author has given the publisher a list of them. Why not? Inefficiency. What can you do about it? Little, except perhaps to find out beforehand if you can when your publisher is going to reprint the book again, and send the production manager a repeat list of the corrections in good time and ask him to ensure that they are carried out.

It is a terrible hassle to get the illustrations for my book, and permission to use them, to say nothing of being extremely expensive. Surely this should be the publisher's responsibility.

It seems to me that in most cases it should be the author's responsibility rather than the publisher's, but the most important thing is that the question of who obtains illustrations and permission for their use (and the same applies to quoted material, to an index, to any extraneous material which is not the author's own work) should be clearly settled before the book is signed up, and the agreed arrangements should be incorporated in the contract. If the obtaining of permission is likely to be a serious financial burden to the author, then this point should be discussed in advance and the publisher may agree to share in the costs or to make some adjustment to his terms to help the author – but he is unlikely to do so unless the situation is made clear to him.

It is important, incidentally, to make sure if you are obtaining permission to reproduce material, whether it is illustrative or textual, that you get permission for the appropriate territories. Your publisher should make clear to you whether he requires clearance for world use or only for the British exclusive market and the open market, and he will need to be specific about the territories concerned. These details can make a great difference to the fees.

The jacket design is a travesty of my book

Increasingly, contracts with publishers, especially those negotiated by agents, include a clause giving the author the right of consultation over the jacket design. Why do publishers resist this? For two reasons, the first being that they believe (sometimes with justice) that they know more about how to sell their books (and the jacket is an important factor in that process) than the author, and secondly because if the author has to be consulted the publisher may be subjected to long arguments and additional delays.

If you are consulted, you should try to restrict your criticism to matters of fact, such as discrepancies between the illustration and the descriptions in your book, and only if you feel very strongly indeed about the design as a whole should you attempt to veto it. You may have the right of consultation, but the publisher has control. If he has any sense, he will listen to you, provided that you are reasonable.

Of course, the most frequent cause of complaint concerns fiction and is that the artist has not followed your descriptions of the characters or the scene which he has portrayed. Really good jacket artists understand that they should reflect the contents of the book, but there are many who feel that they have licence to adapt in order to make what they consider a better picture, and this is why, for instance, your blue-eyed blonde heroine may turn up on the jacket looking like a Spanish señorita. Why doesn't the publisher make the artist change his painting? Usually because to do so would seriously delay publication of the book – but that, it seems to many, is a poor excuse. Other problems arise from a practice of some publishers of buying stacks of artwork with no particular book in mind; when a jacket has to be prepared, the art director looks through his available artwork and chooses something which is often no more than vaguely appropriate. It's a poor way of working, and the author is entitled to make a strong protest.

My book has been very badly produced, on poor paper and in small print

Publishers insist that the manner in which they produce books is their responsibility alone. Sometimes, in their efforts to economize and keep the retail price of the book down, they go too far, and the result is a very unattractive volume. Whether, unless the book is quite ludicrously unpleasing or is physically difficult to read, this will affect the sales, it is hard to say. Books can be very beautiful objects, and some people collect them as such, but the majority are bought to be read, and ugly though some of them may be, are in fact read, if they have something worthwhile to say.

I have to wait a ridiculously long time between delivery of the typescript and publication

Most authors quickly accustom themselves to the fact that there is normally a long delay between the acceptance of their typescript and publication. The reasons why publishing seems to be such a slow process are explained in Chapter 4. What is more worrying is the postponement of scheduled publication. The most frequent cause of this is that there has been some unforeseen delay in the manufacturing process – perhaps the printer has not kept to his schedule, or the paper for the book has been discovered to be faulty, or there has been a strike, or editorial work on the book has taken much longer than anticipated. If the publisher can give you a reasonable explanation of what has caused the delay, then you can only accept it with as good a grace as you can manage. If he cannot explain it to your satisfaction, you have few courses of action open. You can decide to leave him, you can sue him for breaking his contract, or you can, after protesting, go away to lick your wounds.

By and large, publishers do not want to delay publication of their books, however difficult that may sometimes be to believe, since the sooner the book is published the sooner they can begin to recoup the money they have spent on it.

My biography of X has been delayed so long by my publisher that another author's biography of the same person has come out first and taken all the attention and sales

A very difficult problem. Delays happen for all sorts of reasons, and some books seem to be jinxed in this respect, while others sometimes go through all the publishing processes remarkably quickly. Perhaps the other publisher was aware of your book and speeded his own in order to pre-empt you. If you are aware of a rival book early enough before publication, you should warn your publisher (who is often surprisingly ignorant about what his competitors are doing, publishing often being a very inward-looking business) in the hope that he may be able to get things moving more quickly. Occasionally publishers of rival books will agree to publish at the same time so as to be fair to both, but not everyone agrees that this is a good idea, and most houses will attempt to steal a march if they can. There is not much you can do about it, except to accept the fact that this is a business in which luck or ill-luck plays a tremendous part.

My book has been wrongly categorized by my publisher

In an attempt to group sections of their lists together, publishers will sometimes gather together some rather odd bedfellows. It might, for example, upset an author to find his book listed under "Hobbies" when it is aimed very firmly at a professional market, or his work on astronomy nestling next to a sensational book about ghosts. Such categorization is, however, unlikely to have any deleterious effect on sales, and the main damage will be to the author's *amour-propre*.

My publisher made a great to-do of consulting me about publicity and promotion, but did not follow it up

The probable reason for failing to follow up the author's suggestions is lack of money. The publicity department's budget is frequently altered by intervention from higher authority in the firm, which sees a cut in publicity spending as the first and easiest of economies in times of difficulty, or by outside influences such as inflation, or by such circumstances as the addition to the list at the last moment of a book on which a great deal of attention and money is to be spent. Or it may be that the suggestions were not followed up because the notes were misfiled or forgotten, or for some equally irritating example of inefficiency.

Without a written undertaking from the publisher, there is nothing much you can do in these circumstances, unless you have the money and the facility to provide your own publicity. If you do decide to do anything like that, tell your publisher first, just to make sure that you do not duplicate efforts.

There is one other point to be made here, and it is an important one since it can apply to a great many aspects of the author's relationship with his publisher's staff. When an editor, or a publicity manager, or a royalties clerk, or the managing director, or the postboy talks to an author, there is usually a desire to be friendly and to please the writer, and it is therefore very much easier at the time, especially for the inexperienced, to promise the author everything rather than possibly have a row by saying "no". Without wanting to add anything to the mistrust which so often unfortunately exists between authors and publishers, I would caution you to take a grain of salt with what your publisher tells you, especially if the person concerned is clearly inexperienced. If you have doubts, ask for a commitment in writing. Whatever it is may still not be carried out, but you would then have legitimate grounds for complaint and for asking that the situation should be remedied.

My book is not advertised, and of course, since it has not been advertised in them, none of the national papers has reviewed it

Few publishers will concede that advertising, especially in the National Press, which is very expensive, actually sells books. The literary editors of national newspapers would strongly deny that the space devoted to a particular publisher's books is directly related to the amount of money he spends in advertising his wares in that paper. See also p. 77.

My book has received no reviews

Only a tiny number of books receive reviews in large numbers. Space for reviews in newspapers and other media is strictly limited and since many literary editors believe that the most important part of their function is to see that "important" books (i.e. literary works and books by authors with well-known names) are reviewed, the chances of notices for less important books, especially popular fiction, are poor. See also p. 80.

All my reviews have been unfavourable

Don't expect your publisher to do anything about this. A protest to the literary editors of the papers concerned will do nothing. If the reviews are inaccurate, you may wish to write to the paper pointing out the reviewer's errors, but this frequently results only in a reply from him in which you suffer still more. Obviously you cannot let a gross distortion of the facts about your book go by, but on the whole it is probably wisest to put up with it if you get bad reviews, consoling yourself with the thought that any publicity is better than none (which isn't necessarily true, of course). You might also stop to wonder whether all the unfavourable notices are in fact justified.

My publisher doesn't send me copies of the reviews of my book

He is not contractually obliged to do so. Most publishers subscribe to a cutting service (which authors can also do if they are wealthy enough to feel it worthwhile), and can often be persuaded to make a photocopy of reviews or to send the author duplicates if they have them. Some publishers send the author all the reviews a certain time after the publication of the book in question, keeping a record only of the quotable words, and clearing their files by this method. If your publisher does not send you reviews, then all you can really do is to ask him to do so.

My book is not available in bookshops

Every publisher is constantly bombarded by letters and phone calls from authors complaining that their books cannot be found in bookstores, particularly the author's local bookshop, or that their friends have not been able to buy copies. Sometimes this is the publisher's fault, but not always. There is nothing that compels any bookseller to stock any given book, not even the fact that the author lives in the same town. All the publisher and his representative can do is to try to persuade the bookseller to order copies. If he refuses, then you and your friends are going to be disappointed.

Of course, publishers are sometimes to blame – they lose orders, they supply the wrong books, they make all kinds of human errors – but by and large they do not refuse to send books to booksellers without good reason. Books lying in warehouses do no good for publishers, but only cost money. Believe it or not, publishers do actually want to sell books, because it is the only way that they can recoup their outlay in publishing books and gather in the money which will pay the author's royalties, and their wages and overhead expenses and perhaps make them a profit which will enable them to stay in business. "What about their income from subsidiary rights?" you may ask. Well, that certainly helps, but it is almost invariably of much less importance than the income from sales of copies of the book. "By their fruits shall ye know them" certainly applies to publishing; successful publishers attract new books and new authors, and the one recipe for success is to sell books in large quantities.

Don't, therefore, immediately blame your publisher if your book is apparently not available in the bookshops. He may be tearing his hair over the situation just as much as you are. The distribution of books, the full penetration of the potential market, is the greatest problem any publisher has to face, not excluding such perennial favourites as cash flow and Difficult Authors. What is the potential market for a book, and how do you reach it? Let us take a typical example. You have written a book on Pig-Sticking, and you tell your publisher of the huge demand there will be for it. "There are five thousand members of the Pig-Sticking Society for whom it will be required reading," you say. "Then there are some ten thousand occasional pig-stickers in Britain and the overseas markets, who are less committed, but still interested – let's say that half of them will buy the book. At least a thousand copies will go to people in the Anti-Pig-Sticking League, who will want to read it so that they know what our latest thinking is. Add in your own standard market, through bookshops and libraries, and it seems to me that you will end up with a printing quantity of at least 15,000 copies." The publisher tries to disillusion you, explaining that the vast majority of your totally committed pig-sticking enthusiasts will not in fact buy the book, but will borrow it, either from each other, or more likely from the public library, which is also where the members of the Anti-Pig-Sticking League will undoubtedly go, if they bother at all. Pressed by you, he may agree that there is in fact a realistic specialist market potential of some 2,000 copies. But how does he reach them? Even if he sends each of the sixteen thousand people from whom these two thousand buyers will come an order form to pass to their local bookseller, there is little likelihood that they will take any action (the average response to a mailing shot is not much more than 1%), and if they are persuaded to go to a bookshop, the bookseller may well have declined to order the book in the first place, and the customer may be so put off by not finding the book readily available that he may give up all idea of buying it. Or it may be that the bookseller to whom that customer goes is one that the publisher has decided that he will no longer supply, perhaps because the bookseller neglects to pay his bills, or regularly breaks the net book agreement, or indulges in early selling (i.e. having a book on sale before its publication date), or for some other valid reason.

But why should the bookseller be so reluctant to order the book? Well, for example, the last time that something similar came along, he was persuaded to take a dozen copies, because the author lived nearby and swore that he had twelve friends who had promised to buy the book. One of them bought the book from that bookseller and two others borrowed that copy, one bought it from a different shop, three got it out of the library, two bought the bookclub edition, two decided to wait until a paperback came out, and one didn't ever intend to read the book anyway. The bookseller was left with eleven unsold copies. That was all right, you might think, since he had bought the books on sale or return and could send back the unsold copies for credit. "Yes," the bookseller would reply, "but while the books were in my shop they were taking up space that I could have devoted to other books that would have sold. Sale or return arrangements help me, but they are the lesser of two evils, and I do my best to order only those books that I am sure of selling."

A fact which does not make the life of the publisher's sales manager any easier is that authors seem always to believe everything that booksellers tell them. Good booksellers do not lie, but others, more prone to human weaknesses, may decide that it is simpler to deal with a dissatisfied customer, especially if he is an author who does not actually want to buy copies of his book, but only to see that they are on display, by putting the blame on the publisher, saying that his order hasn't been filled or even that he has been told that the book is out of print. And we have all met the incompetent bookseller's assistant who seems to have no knowledge of the wares in the shop or any desire to serve customers, and who will say anything which will get an awkward inquirer out of the shop and leave him in peace. If you have a complaint about your book not being available, be prepared to ask your publisher whether what you have been told is true, before you go off the deep end. And it will help if you can name the bookshop concerned, and report accurately what has been said.

I do not want, on the other hand, to put all the blame on booksellers, large numbers of whom do a very good job. Imagine being faced with close on forty thousand new books every year, plus the necessity of keeping stocks of backlist books and standard works such as Bibles and dictionaries. Small wonder that they do not stock all books. Naturally, the larger the bookshop the better chance there is of finding your book in it, and if it is not there, the large bookseller may find it easier to order copies than his smaller *confrère*, because he can do so directly from the publisher, whereas the small shop will probably get books from a wholesaler – but this latter method can, if you are lucky, provide a fast and efficient service.

It is particularly galling, of course, when your book is not available in the shops for some special occasion, especially as such events do often help to sell books and are ephemeral in nature, so that the sales won't be achieved when the books eventually arrive, as they frequently do, two or three days after the whole thing is over. There is nothing you can do, except to complain loudly and hope that your publisher won't be so inefficient in future.

"But why," you may ask in justifiable exasperation, "is it apparently so difficult to get books speedily from the publisher to the bookshop, sometimes taking five or six weeks?" First of all, it may be that the bookseller has not sent your order off immediately, not because he is inefficient (though that could also be a reason for delay), but because it makes considerable economic sense for everyone concerned, even including the customer, who may avoid having to pay a surcharge on a single copy order, if the bookseller lumps together the orders he receives for books which have to be ordered from one particular source. Next there is the question of delays in the post, which we all suffer from time to time, especially with second-class mail. When the order arrives in the publisher's office, it may not be entirely clear and may have to be referred back to the bookseller, but even without that complication it may have to take its place in a queue of orders waiting to be processed, and similarly when the invoice and packing instructions reach the warehouse, it may not be possible to deal with the order immediately. At any one of these stages additional time may be lost if weekends happen to be awkwardly placed in relation to the progress of the order, and holidays and illnesses can also cause delay. Nevertheless, some publishers manage to be far more efficient than others in processing orders. Why? Well, it may be that the efficiency is produced by employing many more staff and by always using first-class post, and by other such practices which can speed the processing of orders, but which will perhaps prevent the publisher in the end from carrying out that first duty to the author, already quoted earlier in this book, of remaining solvent. Efficiency has to be measured in cost-effectiveness as well as in excellence of service. The truly efficient publishers have better management and staff – it's as simple as that – and very lucky in that respect they are too.

The solution to all these problems is to write an enormous bestseller. It will also remove most of the other causes for complaint dealt with in this chapter. But since for most authors that is just a dream, some more practical advice may be in order. Do let your publisher know if your book is not available in the bookshops, but try to do so in a friendly rather than a complaining way, and don't keep on and on about it. He is probably well aware of whatever is wrong, and is doing what he can to put it right.

If all else fails, some publishers will allow their authors to buy copies of their books for re-sale to their friends. There is a standard clause in most authors' contracts which allows the author to buy copies of the book at trade terms, *but not for re-sale*. If you buy your books from the publisher at trade terms you must therefore have his permission before selling them to your friends. Such sales will presumably be at full retail price and you will make a profit: remember that you will have to declare such earnings to the Inland Revenue. You should also, if your publisher agrees to the arrangement, use it with care, making sure that you do not take sales away from a bookseller by so doing, and if your local bookseller stead-

fastly refuses to stock your book, it might be as well to tell him
that you propose to sell copies yourself.

**I have the feeling that my publisher is only interested in selling
to libraries**

You may be quite right. Some books, particularly in the field
of popular fiction – romances, westerns, and so on – are
published virtually exclusively for the library market, and the
publisher makes little or no effort to sell the titles to bookshops. He doesn't do so because he knows full well that the
bookshops won't order the book. Bookshops in this country,
especially outside London, sell very little fiction, and that
applies to so-called "literary" novels as well as to "entertainment" fiction. Apart from the work of a limited number of
bestselling authors, fiction sells in hardcover in Britain almost
exclusively to libraries. You need to be realistic. If your
publisher sees your book as one for the library market and
makes no effort in other directions, he is almost certainly
right. He is also possibly a specialist in that kind of publishing,
so before you rush off to another house, which does try to sell
to outlets other than libraries, make sure that you're really
going to be better off.

**My publisher's firm is so small that his books are not distri-
buted by the major chains such as W. H. Smith**

A problem indeed, for the publisher as well as the author, and
one to which I can offer no solution. If your book is of a very
specialist nature, it may not matter a great deal that it is not
available in the major chains, provided that your publisher
knows how to sell it in its own market, but if it is a general
book, its chances may well be damaged. There is always the
hope that the small firm will get bigger, or produce such
stunning books that the chains have to take its output.

My previous books have always sold more copies

This does not mean necessarily that your publisher is making
any less effort – indeed, he may be trying harder than ever in
the past. The plain fact is that over the last twenty years or
more the market for hardcover books has declined and
continues to decline.

My publisher refuses to reprint my book

Publishing is a chancy business. No one can predict for certain how a new book will perform – whether it will sell as expected or in excess of or below its target. Fixing print quantities for books is a gamble. Many factors are considered: the publisher's experience with books of a similar nature, the editor's enthusiasm, the reaction of subsidiary rights buyers prior to publication, the jacket, advance orders from bookshops, and of course some kind of estimate of the book's potential, and so on. It is very difficult to get the answer right, and failure to set print quantities at the exact level to obtain all possible sales without being left with an overstock is the reason why publishers, as a whole, are not wealthy men, and why their businesses are particularly vulnerable in adverse trade conditions. More often than not the publisher is over-optimistic and prints too many copies, and has to remainder or pulp the surplus, almost always losing money on such copies. Many years ago, conditions were much easier; it was the habit to bind small quantities of the printed sheets of a book, binding more as and when the demand came along, thus minimizing the amount of capital tied up in finished stock; moreover, it was not uneconomic to keep quantities of a book available over a long period of time, even though sales were very slow. Nowadays, the whole of an edition is normally printed and bound at one time, and the storage of books is an extremely expensive business. Books which do not sell quickly cannot be allowed to take up valuable warehouse space, and in an effort to avoid overstocks, the publisher will sometimes print too few copies. The book sells out on publication or shortly thereafter, and the author is then dismayed when the publisher refuses to reprint. Why does he do so? Usually because the information that he gathers from his sales representatives and from bookshops leads him to believe that the unsatisfied demand is not large enough to warrant reprinting, which cannot be done economically for anything but a large quantity, often virtually as big as the original print run. Although the charges for setting the book in type have been met, and the initiation of artwork and illustrations has been paid for, the cost of putting the plates back on the printing machine and of doing all the other things necessary to manufacture the reprint is so high that a large printing is needed if the unit cost per book is to be kept to a level which will be profitable. This is one of the reasons why authors whose sales have brought them to a higher scale of royalties are asked to revert to a minimal royalty on "small" reprints of 1,500 or sometimes 2,000 copies or less. The more elaborate the book, especially if colour illustrations are involved, the more costly the origination of the reprint will be.

Sometimes the sales reports will suggest that there is sufficient demand to justify a reprint, but that it will take many years before the entire quantity is sold, and the publisher may regretfully have to decide that he cannot tie up the required capital for that length of time.

Knowing all this does not console the author who sees lost sales (and the publisher will not be happy about it either), but at least he can feel sure that the publisher is more likely to be receptive to his next book than if he had over-printed the first one.

My book is to be remaindered

When the sale of a book has stopped or has petered down to almost nothing, the publisher is often left with a stock of unsaleable books. The growth of the paperback market has largely taken away from the hardcover publisher his ability to produce cheap editions (which in the distant past were often simply the original edition made available at a lower price), and his usual practice is to "remainder" the book, that is to say, to sell off the remainder of his stock at a low price, which is usually below his manufacturing cost. The merchant who buys this "remainder" stock then markets it to the public at bargain prices. Apart from the problem of whether or not the author receives any royalty on remainder sales (see p. 116), the author is often angered because his book has been remaindered within too short a period of original publication. The justice in this matter depends to some extent on the kind of book involved, and it seems to me that if one is talking of a serious work of non-fiction which is not essentially topical and ephemeral, it is entirely reasonable for the prohibition to remain in force that the book shall not be remaindered until a minimum of two years after its first publication. If for some reason, however, the book has stopped selling, even in such cases the author might agree to remaindering, trusting that his publisher would not advocate such a course if he believed that he could make more money by keeping the book alive on his list – which he will surely do if the sales income is going to bring him even a small profit as opposed to the almost certain loss of remaindering. But the author's consent should be sought.

If, however, we are considering fiction, it is an unfortunate truth that the majority of novels are virtually moribund six months after publication. If the publisher wishes to remainder your novel within a comparatively short period, though you might well ask him to keep it going for a few months longer, or perhaps to remainder only a part of his stock so that he still has copies available through normal trade channels, it seems to me reasonable for you to consider his request favourably. You may say that he should make a renewed sales effort to dispose of the overstocks, but this just does not work, unless there is some outside influence to affect matters, such as the release of a film of the book. Booksellers, faced with scores of new books appearing every month, will not look kindly on the attempt to sell them a novel which they first considered six months or more ago, and which cannot be said to have exactly leapt off the shelves.

Authors are also incensed, and rightly so, when their books are remaindered without their knowledge. If the book is to be remaindered, the author should always have the opportunity of buying copies at the remainder price, and it is outrageous that some books are sold off in this way without the author being told. Unfortunately, by the time he discovers what has happened, it is usually too late to do anything about it, but a vigorous protest to the publisher has sometimes resulted in the latter at least buying back from the remainder merchant the number of copies that the author wants.

I was not told of the bookclub sale until the royalty statement arrived

You are right to feel annoyed. It's bad-mannered and stupid of your publisher not to have told you something like that, especially as it was good news. How did it happen? Well, the subsidiary rights manager probably thought the editor was writing to you, and the editor thought the sub-rights person was writing . . . and in the end no one wrote. Protest, and ask that nothing similar should happen in future.

162   *An Author's Guide to Publishing*

My publisher has sold his own edition of my book in the United States rather than selling the rights to an American publisher

This situation normally applies only to highly illustrated books, especially those which have a number of pages in full colour. The only way in which the book can be made economic is for the British and American publishers to work together so that a double-sized print quantity can be ordered. Books of British origin are manufactured in such cases by the British publisher, who usually sells the sheets to the American publisher at a fairly low price which is inclusive of royalty, and the same thing works in reverse with books of American origin. Sometimes foreign language editions are also involved. The reward to the author on these deals is minimal, but it is often true that if no such arrangement could be worked out, the book would not be published on either side of the Atlantic, and this is why in many cases the British (or American) publisher will not sign a firm contract with the author until he has sold an edition of the book to an American (or British) publisher.

If there is no such cost problem and it is a perfectly ordinary book, it is surprising that the British publisher should try to sell his own edition in the States, and he is unlikely to have much success. However, if he has tried unsuccessfully to sell the American rights, a few extra sales of his own edition are better than nothing.

No effort has been made to sell subsidiary rights in my book

Are you sure? If your publisher has really made no effort to sell subsidiary rights, he is either a fool or incompetent, and you should leave him if you can find someone else to take you on, and providing your contract allows you to do so. But do try to find out first whether it is simply that, despite considerable industry on his part, all the subsidiary rights buyers to whom he has submitted your book have rejected it. Paperback publishers, bookclub editors, serial editors for magazines and newspapers are all faced with an embarrassment of riches, and reject far more books than they accept. Some years ago Sir Robert Lusty suggested that only one hardcover book in twenty also achieved bookclub or paperback sales; with the proliferation of bookclubs since then the chances may have improved a little, but would probably not be better than one in fifteen.

If your book has not sold any subsidiary rights, you may have been unlucky, or it may be that your book is just not good enough, but it doesn't necessarily mean that your publisher hasn't tried. If you ask him, he may be able to tell you to whom he has submitted the book and possibly whether they have given any reasons for rejection, and this may be useful information to bear in mind when writing your next book. He may also tell you why he has *not* submitted the book to this or that paperback publisher. If, for instance, the editor of a paperback house has repeatedly told your publisher that he does not want any historical fiction, your publisher would be foolish to send him your historical novel – unless it is of such outstanding quality that he can say to the paperback editor, "I know you don't want historical fiction, but this one is so brilliant that you must read it." If the paperback editor knows that your publisher would not say that unless the book really were extraordinarily good, then he might make an exception and consider it. But if the book is as splendid as that, your publisher will have had no difficulty in selling it to one of the other paperback houses anyway.

My publisher turned down a subsidiary rights offer as not good enough; it has now been withdrawn, and no other offer has come in

Bad luck. I keep telling you it's a gambling business.

It is unfair that I have to wait so long for my share of subsidiary rights income

Publishers who sell subsidiary rights receive moneys from those to whom they sell, and then divide them according to the proportions set out in the contract between themselves and the author. Now, it has been standard practice for many years that the advance originally paid by the publisher to the author is against all sums due under the contract, which means that the author receives no extra payment until the advance has been earned, whether by royalties on the original edition or from the author's share of subsidiary rights, or a combination of the two. Let us suppose that the publisher has paid an advance of £1,000, and has sold subsidiary rights for a sum of which the author's share is £600. £600 of the original advance has now been earned, but that money will not be paid to the author, nor will any further sums be payable until the remaining £400 of the advance has been earned. This is not necessarily unfair, especially since publishers frequently take into account their expectations of receipts from subsidiary rights when calculating how much the original advance should be. But see the proposals for advance payments set out in the Minimum Terms Agreement, discussed in Chapter 5.

What is less fair is the practice of some publishers of retaining the author's share of subsidiary rights moneys *after* the original advance has been fully earned until they next send a royalty statement to the author. This could mean that for a considerable period of time moneys due to the author are kept and used by the publisher. Supposing that after the advance has been earned your publisher sells certain subsidiary rights in your book for a sum of which your share is £500. If his royalty accounting periods end at 30th June and 31st December, and if it so happened that these subsidiary rights moneys came into him on 1st July, he could retain the £500 until the following 31st March, when he would normally be rendering to you the royalty statement for the six months ending 31st December. Many authors' organizations and agents are now insisting that once the advance has been earned, the author's share of any subsidiary rights money should be paid to him by the publisher immediately the publisher receives it.

The hardcover edition of my book is out of print, and the publisher refuses to reprint, but he is still taking his cut of the paperback royalties

Most publishing contracts include a clause which allows the publisher to retain rights provided that any sub-licensed edition of the book is in print, even if his own edition is not. A reprint may be impossible to contemplate, for even though the book may still be selling in the sub-licensed edition, the market for the original edition may now be non-existent or too small to justify the reprint. In these circumstances some publishers will occasionally agree to increase the author's share of the subsidiary income, but very few will release all rights to the author, arguing that the fact that they took the initial risk with the book, and that if they had not done so the subsidiary rights in question would not have been sold at all, and it was they who conducted the negotiations for the sale, is a valid justification for them taking their share, and will remain so throughout the life of the sub-licence in question. Legally, unless your contract does not have the kind of clause referred to above, you have no cause for redress. Morally, it depends somewhat on the kind of sums involved. If the publisher has already received a very substantial sum in the form of his share of subsidiary rights income, then perhaps he has less justification for still taking his full percentage than if the moneys involved are small. But that's a difficult one to argue.

My royalty statements are late and/or inaccurate

Publishers usually make up their royalty statements for a six months period (though some are now moving towards one annual statement only, a move which authors should resist), and then render the statements and make any payments due three months thereafter. Why does it take so long? Chiefly because of the large numbers of active royalty accounts which the average publisher has to deal with, and their complexity. A large publisher may have thousands of books still active on his list, and it takes a considerable time to prepare all the statements, draw the necessary cheques, grouping together all books by one author and all authors represented by any one agent. Moreover, just as every book is different, so its royalty statement will be different, with different royalty rates, different subsidiary rights sales and terms, different charges to be made against the account, and so on. Three months should be sufficient for even the largest publisher to get all the work done, but it is perhaps understandable, if very unfortunate, that in these days of shorter office hours and less dedicated and well-trained staff, some publishers fall down in this respect.

Equally, it is scarcely surprising that some royalty statements are inaccurate. All authors should check their royalty statements carefully, and bring any errors to the notice of their publishers. Some royalty statements are very difficult to understand, and if you have that kind of problem, you should ask your publisher to explain his form in detail. Errors seem more prone to creep in now that many royalty statements are produced on computers, not only because computers (or rather, as the computer manufacturers never tire of telling us, the people who feed in the information) make mistakes, but also because it is extremely difficult to draw up a computer programme which will cover all the enormous variety of accounting that a large publisher has to undertake for his authors.

I am sure that a small advance means no promotion and no effort or, indeed, interest

There is some truth in this, but it isn't the entire story. When a publisher pays a really large sum of money as the advance on a book, it is indeed likely that he will also spend quite a lot on promoting it and he will print a large number of copies, and devote a lot of his time and that of his staff to it. But there are comparatively few such books on any publisher's list, and it does not mean that the rest are neglected. They may not get star treatment (it is not an equal world), but they are nevertheless important to the publisher, who does not live on bestsellers alone. If your publisher doesn't pay an advance of thousands of pounds for your book, then in terms of his effort and interest it really won't matter a great deal whether the advance he pays is £50 or £750 or nothing at all. He is committed to spending a substantial sum on the manufacture of any book on his list, and his desire to recoup his outlay guarantees you at least a modicum of effort and interest. Occasionally a genuine ugly duckling comes along – a book which no one expected to be a big seller, but which suddenly takes off into the realms of success. The amount the publisher paid as an advance doesn't affect his effort and interest in that book, and since the advance was small, the author's first royalty cheque is all the nicer.

My book was published six months ago, but already my publisher has lost interest in it

In most cases, a very high proportion of the sales of a book has been achieved before and within six months of publication, and thereafter sales may virtually have ceased. Additional promotion and effort by the publisher will not stimulate additional sales, unless there is some justification for it, such as the release of a film based on the book. Even then, the new publicity may result only in the sale of those copies of the book already in the bookshops, without much re-ordering. Books which survive for a longer period usually continue to sell on their own momentum, and again additional attention does not often produce much effect.

Your publisher's lack of interest in your book is largely due to the fact that he is concerned with the new books on his list. He has to keep on producing new books and his attention is bound to be focused on them.

Whenever I complain to my publisher, he just fobs me off with some unconvincing explanation

This sounds like a rather unhappy situation. Either the publisher is incompetent and does not know the answers to your queries, and hasn't the courage to tell you that he doesn't know, or more likely he is ashamed of his firm's inefficiency and is trying to cover up. Loyalty to his firm and to his colleagues may be preventing him from confessing how right you are and how justified your complaints. Not only that, but to tell you the truth might mean that you would lose any remaining faith in the firm that you might have. I think he's wrong, and that honesty is always the best policy for a publisher in dealing with his authors.

Of course, the trouble might be that you are a Difficult Author . . . .

My publisher is greedy

Very probably. If you think so, tell him. He may be able to explain to you why he appears that way; he may even respond by being more generous towards you. But do remember that one of his functions is to help make his firm profitable, and that may mean saving as much money as is consistent with not losing good publishing opportunities as a result of apparent parsimony. Don't blame him for trying to strike a good bargain. Try a little haggling.

8
The Rewards of Writing

Every now and then considerable publicity is given to the success story of certain bestselling authors. We learn of the astronomic sums paid in the United States for the paperback rights to their books, we are told of colossal sales of the film rights, we hear they themselves have had to become tax exiles. No wonder many people think that writing is an easy way of making money. Most of them never get beyond thinking about it, but if they do try to write they are likely to discover that it is much harder work and demands far more skill than they thought. And of course, it is not just a matter of putting all those thousands of words on paper – there is also the business of planning and construction (which is what we are doing, as all we authors know, when we are discovered apparently asleep at our desks). Oh, yes, it is very hard, and the skills are not easily acquired.

But there is another shock waiting for our friend who thinks that writing is an easy way of making money, for if he manages to complete a book and get it accepted for publication, he will discover that the average author's earnings are pitifully small, and that very few can make writing a full-time career unless they have means of some other kind.

Perhaps our friend will have some little success with his first book, and will then believe that his future as an author is assured. But he will find that earning his living from writing is a totally uncertain business. His next book may be a failure and he may never be published again. He may write a number of books and eventually have the right to consider himself as "established", but his income from his writing may still vary from book to book and from year to year quite unpredictably. Even if he becomes a household name, he will probably need a whole string of bestsellers before he can feel certain that anything else he writes will automatically bring him in a large and steady income. But he's more likely anyway to be one of the thousands to whom their books bring no more than pin money.

So what are the rewards of writing? First of all, and despite the fact that I can hear some of my readers giving a hollow laugh, there is the reward of writing for its own sake. Almost all authors like to talk about the agony of writing, but though it is certainly very hard work and requires considerable stamina and application, I have yet to find an author who really and truly finds his work an agony. On the contrary, most will admit, if pressed, to the pleasure it gives them. There is a sense of achievement in putting words to paper, a joy in the creativity involved, and there can sometimes be great happiness in reading something that you have written and finding satisfaction in it, feeling that you have managed to express exactly what you were intending to say, and in the best possible manner.

When, earlier in this book, I replied cynically to the statement that everyone has a book in him by saying that it should usually stay there, I was really making a commercial judgement; "everyone" more often than not has neither an interesting enough story nor the skill with which to tell it to make the book a likely candidate for publication. But my cynicism ignores that simple pleasure which "everyone" may get just from writing his story, so if you have never written before, but believe there is a book inside you, then go ahead and bring it out.

Few authors, except perhaps for ardent diarists, and even they may have half an eye on the main chance, write only for themselves. Again there can be rewards, even if your writing remains unpublished, for it may give great pleasure to your family and friends. I think particularly of those autobiographies with which every publisher is familiar, which do not get published because their authors are unknown and their lives neither unusual enough nor distinguished enough to be of wide, and saleable, interest. Those stories will probably be of great value to the family. Don't we all regret how little we know of our grandparents and the generations before them?

So if this is the kind of book you think of writing, do go ahead – write it for your own enjoyment and that of your family. Don't expect to be published commercially, though of course there is no harm in trying to interest a publisher, and if you succeed in that, you will have earned yourself a nice bonus. Or if you write poetry or science fiction or treatises on

unpronounceable chemical compounds or a manual of Pig
Sticking, or even an account of your package holiday in Playa
El Populario, Majorca, or the hilarious story of your house-
moving – whatever you write, don't let anyone stop you or
discourage you, and above all don't be too disappointed if you
do not achieve publication. Remember that there are other
rewards in writing.

However, you are probably still interested in the financial
question. Let us suppose that you have something to say, are
equipped to say it, and that it is of book length. (By "something to say", I do not mean necessarily that you have to have
some sort of message for the world, but that you have a story
to tell, or information to impart; by "equipped to say it", I
mean that you have a modicum of writing ability, can express
your thoughts on paper, perhaps have some understanding of
the shape and form that a book requires, and the stamina to
complete it; and by "book length", I mean that, unless it falls
into a category such as children's books or poetry where much
shorter lengths are acceptable, the typescript when completed would be at least thirty to thirty-five thousand words in
length.) So you write your book, and then have the good
fortune to find a publisher who agrees to publish it. What can
you expect to earn from it?

I cannot tell you. You could make a fortune, or you might
barely cover your expenses, or end up out of pocket. You are
likely to receive an advance from your publisher which might
be as little as £50, or a more reasonable £500, or, if your
publisher accepts the Minimum Terms Agreement (see Chapter 5) and the book is of average length and of general
interest, it might be as much as £1,000, or even £1,500. The
advance could equally be in a much higher bracket if the
publisher can envisage a really large sale, or if he is using the
"advance against all earnings" formula (see p. 112) and is
reasonably certain of making sales of subsidiary rights for
substantial sums.

If the advance is low, you will have some chance of earning
royalties which exceed it, but remember that for a book
priced at £5, one thousand copies have to be sold at a royalty
of 10% to earn you £500, and many books nowadays fail to
reach that sales figure in the home market. If the paperback
rights are sold, the paperback publisher will probably pay an
advance of upwards of £250, but you will share those moneys
with your hardcover publisher in proportions determined in

your contract (see p. 116). Translations may bring in extra sums, and if the US rights in your book are sold, the increase in your earnings could vary from modest to substantial. But it is all extremely chancy, and if you end up making £1,500 out of your book you have been far from unlucky. When you consider the fact that you have spent a great deal of time and effort in writing the book, and that the income does not usually arrive in one nice cheque, but may be spread over a long period – even several years – it is plain that you are not going to be rich. Even if you multiply those earnings by ten, meaning that you have had a fairly substantial success, it will probably take at least four years from the time you began to write until you have received the whole of the £15,000, so it scarcely adds up to a princely annual income.

Many authors see their salvation in PLR (Public Lending Right), under which authors will receive some payment according to the popularity of their books in public libraries, but, as has already been mentioned, the amounts earned are unlikely, unless you are already in the bestseller class, to be very impressive and will hardly keep you from starvation if your writing is your only source of income. The PLR scheme is of course very welcome, but we must hope that in time it will be improved.

Incidentally, certain foreign countries operate their own PLR and British authors, whether their books are translated into the languages concerned or not, may benefit from the schemes. In order to do so, you should join ALCS (The Author's Lending and Copyright Society Limited), an agency which is authorized to collect and distribute the moneys concerned. For information, write to: The Secretary General, The Authors' Lending and Copyright Society Ltd, 430 Edgware Road, London W2 1EH. ALCS is also to be the distribution agency for moneys due to authors under the proposed Copyright Licensing Authority, which will issue licences and collect fees for the photocopying of copyright material.

It cannot be repeated too often that bestsellerdom is not always solely a question of your ability as a writer, important though that is, but also depends to a frightening extent on luck – the luck of choosing the right title, finding the right publisher, being published at the right time, receiving the right kind of publicity, finding the public in the right mood to respond to your work. Many potential bestsellers are published every year, of which a few make it to the top, and the others sink without trace – and it is a matter of luck. Certainly some publishers are more vigorous than others in forcing their books on to the bestseller lists, and some authors feel that it is a great advantage to be published by one of the big concerns because of the extra weight they can bring to bear and their flexibility and strength of resources; others believe that it is better to be a large fish in a small pond than a medium-sized or small fish in a big one, and that you get far more personal attention, and therefore perhaps a better chance of becoming a bestseller with a small publishing house. Whichever kind of publisher you have and however hard he may try to make you into a bestseller, he will have to have a little bit of luck – no, a fairly large bit of luck – to succeed.

The element of fortune is something that, if you are wise, you should accept. Some authors are for ever bemoaning their failure to hit the jackpot, frequently blaming their publishers for their lack of success, whereas others content themselves with making a nice little addition to their income by writing and publishing new books regularly, but without hankering too continuously for rewards that they are never likely to earn. They keep their envy of luckier (or perhaps more skilful) authors in check, and allow their dissatisfaction to focus on the quality of their own work – and of course, no good writer is ever satisfied entirely with what he writes. This is not to say that you should have no confidence in yourself and your writing. I think every writer should say to himself every day, "My new book is the best I have ever written – but it won't make me a fortune." The first part of that may help to keep up your morale, while the second half may help to ensure that your bank manager loses no sleep over you.

Bank managers must, very often, dread having authors on their books. They tend to be a feckless lot, who spend their earnings as soon as they receive them (or more often before), and the more money they earn, the more feckless they are likely to be, living extravagantly, divorcing their wives and having to pay enormous sums of alimony, making no provision for tax payments, and generally behaving in money matters with all the financial acumen of a demented Monopoly player. When the bank manager refuses to allow them a further overdraft, or demands repayment of their outstanding loans, or the Inland Revenue Inspector sends them one of his more horrid notices, they go to their publishers, asking for advances on as yet unwritten books, or at least the payment of that part of the advance due on publication of their current work, despite the fact that they have not yet delivered the typescript. Publishers often try to be helpful, especially if the author concerned is a star of great magnitude and they want to keep him on the list, but they are greatly restricted nowadays by the high cost of capital, and may baulk at investing more when the possibility of return on the money is a long way off.

Of course, there are many, many prudent authors who manage their affairs without ever falling into debt, and who take a realistic view of the potential earning capacity of their work. Even when their publishers greet their new book with excited little cries and begin to talk hysterically of enormous sales and US and foreign language and subsidiary rights buyers queuing up for the chance to bid for the book, these sober, sensible authors, instead of cracking a bottle of champagne to celebrate, will take a large pinch of salt with all that is said, and wait to see what happens. If the publisher is right, the champagne will keep for the few months before he is proved so; if he is wrong, a good cup of tea or coffee will be much cheaper and almost as cheering. It goes without saying that I am just such a sensible author, and I am sure that you, who are reading this now, are another.

Remember that any income you receive from writing has to be reported to the Inland Revenue, and you will be taxed on it. If you are a professional author, it is almost essential to get a good accountant, and preferably one who understands something of the author's position *vis-à-vis* the tax authorities. There are many expenses that authors can legitimately claim, such as the cost of writing and typing materials and other stationery, research expenses including the purchase of books for that purpose, postage and telephone including telephone rental, travel and motoring costs, secretarial charges (which can include some remuneration for your spouse who takes messages, checks proofs, helps with research) and so on. Of course, all these costs must be incurred solely for the purpose of your writing, and in the case, for instance, of telephone rental, unless you have a separate business line which you use solely as an author, only a proportion of the charges will be allowable. You should keep all bills and receipts in connection with your writing for your accountant's use. Your accountant will also in certain circumstances be able to arrange for the "spreading" of your

174 An Author's Guide to Publishing

writing income, which to some extent allows you to even out the good and the bad years. Advice on these matters is often available from agents, and the Society of Authors or the Writers' Guild may be able to help, but there is really no substitute for a capable accountant. Few publishers are qualified to give reliable tax advice.

I referred at the beginning of the last paragraph to "professional" authors. If you are writing in your spare time from another job, which provides your main livelihood, can you really consider yourself a professional author? It depends on your attitude. If your whole approach to writing is professional, the fact that it is a spare-time job is irrelevant. Being professional means dedication and perseverance, and a determination never to fall below the highest standards that you can attain.

My favourite quotation about the writing business comes from the American author of humorous, witty novels and verse, Peter de Vries. He says, "I write when I'm inspired, and I see to it that I'm inspired at nine o'clock every morning." It may sound like a joke, but that attitude is symptomatic of real professionalism. It is an attitude which, if true of his approach to all aspects of his work, guarantees to any writer with sufficient talent that he will indeed reap a reward from his efforts.

9

Organizations For Authors

Being an author is often a very lonely business. It is not just that one tends to write in a private world, shut off by the act of creation even from one's family and friends; it is also frequently very difficult to know where to go for unbiased advice regarding one's dealings with publishers, and for the companionship of others whose problems and pleasures may be somewhat similar.

In the matter of advice, it is hoped that this book will be of some help, but it clearly cannot cover every problem that may arise. You may feel that you can rely on your agent for sound advice, but supposing that you want to find out whether he himself is behaving towards you as he should? And if you have no agent anyway, where can you go?

The Society of Authors

The Society of Authors, founded in 1884, exists primarily to further the interests of authors and to defend their rights. It therefore acts as an advisory body to its individual members, but also represents authors' interests in negotiations with Government departments (over such matters as VAT and PLR) and with publishers, either individually or through the Publishers Association, and with any other bodies which may be concerned with authors and their work. It also administers various prizes and funds, and acts for the estates of some deceased authors.

After a referendum of its members, the Society became, in 1978, an independent trade union. It is not affiliated to the TUC, and is completely non-political. Only those members with extremely strong principles against becoming union members found it necessary to resign when the Society took this step.

The Society offers free legal advice and, in some cases,

representation to its members, but does make the rule that it cannot be involved in a legal dispute which is already in existence at the time you join the Society – in other words, if you are in the middle of a legal argument with your publisher, for instance, it is no use rushing off to join the Society of Authors and expecting it immediately to take on your case with all the attendant expenses. If you are already a member and were before the dispute began, that is a different matter. The Society also offers free business advice to its members.

The Society includes a number of specialist sub-organizations: Broadcasting, Children's Writers, Educational Writers, Medical and Technical Groups, and a Translators Association. It publishes a quarterly magazine, *The Author*, and it has available a most useful set of "Quick Guides" to such subjects as Copyright, The Protection of Titles, Income Tax, Libel, Value Added Tax, Publishing Contracts and Authors' Agents, and "Bulletins" on such subjects as Translators as Authors and Teachers as Authors. These leaflets are free to members, and available to others at a modest fee.

The Society of Authors is principally concerned with advisory and representational activities, but it also organizes seminars and other events which combine the useful and the merely social. Full membership is open only to those who have been published, but associate membership is available if you have had a manuscript accepted for publication, or if you have an established reputation in another medium, or if you have contributed occasional scripts to the media. The annual subscription is a set sum (currently £50 in most cases). Full details may be obtained from: The Membership Secretary, The Society of Authors, 84 Drayton Gardens, London SW10 9SD. Telephone: 01-373 6642.

The Writers' Guild of Great Britain

Originally called the Television and Screenwriters Guild, this organization has in recent years widened its scope to include representation for all kinds of authors. There is inevitably a certain area of overlap between the Writers' Guild and the Society of Authors, both organizations working jointly on such issues as Public Lending Right, reprography, and most recently the negotiations concerning the Minimum Terms Agreement for books.

Unlike the Society of Authors, the Writers' Guild is affiliated to the TUC, but states that it is non-political. It is also affiliated to other unions in the Entertainment industries and to the Writers' Guilds in the English-speaking countries around the world.

The Guild's principal aims are twofold. Firstly, to give individual advice and help to members on the whole range of issues involving their business life as writers, including legal advice, taxation and contracts; and secondly, to negotiate minimum terms agreements in each of the five industries using a writer's work. The Guild currently has agreements providing for protection to its members in film, television, radio, theatre and books.

It publishes a monthly Newsletter and the *Writers News*, a quarterly journal.

Membership is open to anyone who has had work published, broadcast or performed, or, importantly, to a first-time writer who has been offered but has not yet signed a contract. The current annual subscription is 1% of a writer's income from writing, with a minimum of £30 and a maximum of £480. Full details are available from the Membership Secretary, The Writers' Guild of Great Britain, 430 Edgware Road, London W2 1EH. Telephone: 01-723 8074.

PEN – The World Association of Writers

This international organization was founded in 1921, and exists to promote and maintain friendship between writers in every country in the interests of freedom of expression and international goodwill. PEN Centres are spread throughout the world; each is autonomous and organizes various seminars and other events for its members, and many of the centres issue regular journals. An International Congress takes place every year. Membership is open to all writers or translators of good standing who agree to support the PEN Charter, without distinction of creed or race. The annual subscription is currently £20 for town members (within fifty miles of London) and £16 for country and overseas members. Full details may be obtained from: PEN International, 7 Dilke Place, London SW3 4JE. Telephone: 01-352 6303.

The Book Trust

Worthy of support by all authors, the Book Trust exists to promote books and reading in any and every possible way. While it receives the support of all branches of the book trade, it is in no way dependent on any of them, and for this reason and because of its charitable status it is able to speak for books to bodies who might be suspicious of a commercial purpose or vested interest. Membership is open to everyone interested in books and reading. The Book Trust (formerly The National Book League) has a useful book information service giving information about books published in the UK and USA; it arranges exhibitions; it has a Children's Book Reference Library and the Mark Longman Library, a collection of books about books, publishing and bookselling. The Trust administers various Literary Awards and book ventures, such as the School Bookshop Association and the National Book Committee. There are varying rates of membership for individuals and for groups or organizations. Membership offers a quarterly magazine, *Booknews*, and use of the Trust facilities, including the Licensed Snack Bar. Full details may be obtained from: The Book Trust, Book House, 45 East Hill, Wandsworth, London SW18 2QZ. Telephone: 01-870 9055.

Writers' Circles

Many authors find congenial companionship in attending Writers' Circles. The membership usually comprises both regularly published authors and those whose work has not appeared in print, and standards of ability are liable to vary greatly within the group. A programme of lectures and social activities is usually arranged, but the reading of new work by members to the assembled company, which is then free to criticize it, is always one of the main functions of the group, and can be very helpful, provided that you are not too thin-skinned. You should be able to find details of your local Circles in the public library. A directory of Writers' Circles is available from: Mrs Jill Dick, Oldacre, Horderns Park Road, Chapel-en-le-Frith, Derbyshire. A similar compilation is to be had from: Mr Bill Stanton, 8 Tewit Well Avenue, Harrogate, N. Yorks HG2 8AP.

Arising out of the Writers' Circle movement and as an extension of their functions, many residential courses for writers take place up and down the country. Fees are usually modest and those who attend find the diet of lectures from experts, discussion groups, brief instructional courses and social activities very much to their taste. The most popular and successful of these residential courses is the Writers' Summer School, which takes place at Swanwick in Derbyshire for a week every August. Full details may be obtained from: The Writers' Summer School, c/o The Red House, Mardens Hill, Crowborough, East Sussex TN6 1XN. Telephone: 08926 3943.

The Arvon Foundation

This organization offers people of all ages over sixteen the chance to meet, talk and work in an informal way with practising artists. The two Arvon centres, one in Yorkshire and one in Devon, provide a full programme of five-day courses in various fields of writing and related art forms. Full details may be obtained from: The Arvon Foundation, Lumb Bank, Heptonstall, Hebden Bridge, West Yorkshire HX7 6DF, or The Arvon Foundation, Totleigh Barton, Sheepwash, Beaworthy, Devon EX21 5NS.

Adult Education Creative Writing Classes

Creative writing classes are of course intended primarily for those who have not been successful in achieving publication, but many successful authors do attend them. Their value naturally depends largely on the ability of the Tutor taking the classes, which in some ways differ from the average Writers' Circle only in that the Tutor is there as a kind of superior authority when the members' work is discussed, though he may devote part of the time to formal lectures. Some people attend the classes more for the sake of a pleasant evening among fellow writers than for the instruction. Details are available from Adult Education offices and from public libraries.

Some other useful organizations:
The Association of British Science Writers, c/o British Association for the Advancement of Science, Fortress House, 23 Savile Row, London W1X 1AB.
The Authors' Club, 40 Dover Street, London W1X 3RB. Telephone: 01-499 8581.

The British Science Fiction Association Limited, c/o 18 Gordon Terrace, Blantyre, Scotland G72 9NA.

The British Guild of Travel Writers, c/o 31 Riverside Court, Caversham, Reading, Berks RG4 8AL. Telephone: (0734) 481384.

The Crime Writers' Association, P.O. Box 172, Tring, Herts HP23 5LP.

The Guild of Travel Writers, 25 Oak Field Road, London N3 2HT. Telephone: 01-346 3772.

The Institute of Journalists, Bedford Chambers, Covent Garden, London WC2E 8HA. Telephone: 01-836 6541.

The National Union of Journalists, Acorn House, 314 Gray's Inn Road, London WC1X 8DP. Telephone: 01-278 7916.

The Poetry Society (Incorporated), 21 Earls Court Square, London SW5 9BY. Telephone: 01-373 7861.

The Romantic Novelists Association, c/o 20 First Avenue, Amersham, Bucks HP7 9BJ.

The Society of Women Writers and Journalists, c/o 3 Nettle-croft, Hemel Hempstead, Herts HP1 1PQ.

Glossary

Advance The moneys paid to an author in advance and on account of the earnings of his book. Normally non-returnable. Often referred to in the USA as a "guarantee".

Back list After a book is first published it becomes, if it continues to sell, part of its publisher's back list. A publisher cannot exist on the sales of new books alone, but is constantly looking for books which will sell over a period of years – i.e. potential back list titles.

Bastard title Another term for "half-title" q.v.

Biblio-page The page of a book which contains the copyright notice, the printing history of the book, the printer's imprint, etc. It is usually on the back, or verso, of the title-page.

Binding Hardcover books are usually bound by being sewn and cased, i.e. the signatures are sewn together and a stiff binding is then attached by means of the end papers. Paperbacks are more often "perfect bound", i.e. the back edges of the signatures are trimmed, so that each page is separate, then glued and the stiff paper cover is then drawn on.

Bleeding Illustrations which go off the edge of the page, so that there is no surround to the illustration, are said to "bleed".

Blocks In letterpress printing, illustrations and diagrams are usually printed from blocks. Line blocks are used where tones or shades of colour are not required. Half-tone blocks are used for photographs and drawings which include, for instance, washes, or which are to be reproduced in full colour.

Blues See Ozalids.

Blurb The material about a book which the publisher prints in his catalogue and on the flap of the jacket. The blurb usually describes the content of the book and assesses its merits. Since the blurb is designed to sell the book it cannot always be relied upon to be entirely truthful.

Boards   The stiff cardboard used in binding a hardcover book. As a descriptive term in a catalogue, "boards" means that the book has a hardcover binding (the boards often being covered with a decorative paper), but no jacket.

Camera-ready copy   Many printing processes involve photography, for which material has to be produced which is error-free, with everything correctly positioned as it is to appear on the page, and which can therefore be called "camera-ready copy".

Cancel page   A page inserted in a printed book in place of a page which contains an error or other material which it is essential to change, even at the cost of this expensive process.

Case   The binding of a hardcover book.

Case   The tray in which type is stored, the upper part containing capital letters and the lower part small letters. "Upper case" has become a synonym for capitals and "lower case" for small letters.

Cast off   A word count usually prepared in a publisher's production department or by a printer. Calculated with care, the object is to work out as accurately as possible the number of printed pages that the book in question will occupy, given a specified type size and type area.

Cloth   Nearly all hardcover books used to be bound in real cloth – a woven fabric. Nowadays, "cloth" is more often a special kind of paper, frequently embossed with a pattern to give the impression that it is the genuine article.

Co-edition   A book produced simultaneously for two or more publishers and for different areas of the world, or languages, in order to reduce printing costs.

Colophon   A publisher's sign or trademark.

Composition   The setting up of type. Methods used include: Monotype, a system in which each letter is cast separately when the compositor presses the key; Linotype, when the casting is not done until the compositor has completed each line; computer typesetting, in which the copy is transferred to a tape which, fed into the computer, produces film of the composition.

Cover   See Jacket.

Double spread   When an illustration runs across two facing pages, without other illustrations on the same pages, it is called a "double spread". The same term may be applied to a publisher's advertisement on two facing pages of, for instance, *The Bookseller*, or to two facing pages devoted to one book in a catalogue.

Dummy   A book made of the paper to be used in the finished article, and bound in the style that will be used for the book, but without the pages being printed. The dummy is used, among other things, for the preparation of the jacket, since it shows the size of the book, including the width of the spine. Dummies are sometimes prepared with a few pages of printed material, especially in the case of highly illustrated books, to give foreign publishers and bookbuyers an impression of what the final book will look like.

Edition   An edition of a book is not the same as an impression. Each impression of the book, that is to say the first and subsequent printings, contains the same material. Each edition, on the other hand, is altered substantially from the previous edition.

Em   A unit of measurement in printing. Since it is based on the width of the letter "m", its size obviously can vary with the size of the type. However, the term is frequently taken to mean a standard 12pt "m", equalling roughly ⅙ inch. See also Point.

End papers   The four pages at the beginning and end of a hardcover book by means of which the case is attached.

Flap   The part of the jacket which is folded inside the cover of the book. "Back flap" and "front flap" are terms which are frequently used.

Folded and collated   After printing, the sheets of paper are folded into signatures, and the signatures are collated or gathered into groups, so that each group contains all the signatures which make up the book.

Folio   The page number.

Format   The size and shape of a book.

Gutter   The "join" where two facing pages of a book meet.

Half-title   A page of a book on which is printed the title of the book, or the title of a Part (in which case it should really be called a "part-title"), but which does not normally carry the author's name or that of the publisher.

Half-tone   The reproduction of photographs or other illustrations involving tone by the letterpress method of printing requires the use of half-tone blocks. The illustrations are broken down into a series of small dots of varying sizes, the larger dots producing the darker areas of the illustration and the smaller ones the lighter area.

ISBN These initials stand for International Standard Book Number. A world-wide system of identifying books by means of a ten-digit number. The first digit identifies the book's country of origin, the next four the publisher, the next four the individual title, and the final number is a check digit.

Imposition The arrangement of the pages for printing so that when the sheet is folded the pages will appear in their correct sequence.

Impression A printing of a book. New impressions of a book are reprints without changes having been made to the content. See also Edition.

Imprint The publisher's name printed at the foot of the title-page is his "imprint". The printer's imprint, consisting of his name and address, is usually printed at the foot of the biblio or imprint page.

In print Books which are "in print" are available from the publisher, as opposed to those which have sold out and will not be reprinted and are designated "out of print". The phrase "in print" is also used to indicate the number of copies printed of a book since it was first published – "There are fifty thousand copies of this book in print, made up of nine impressions", or "I have published ten of this author's books, totalling over two million copies of his works in print in paperback editions."

Jacket Sometimes called "dust jacket" or "dust cover" or "wrapper". The loose paper cover on a hardcover book, often carrying an illustration on the front and a blurb and the retail price on the front flap. Paperbacks do not normally have jackets, and their stiff paper bindings are known as "covers".

Leading Space between lines of type.

Letter spacing Space between the letters of a word, often used when the word is set entirely in capitals, as in a title.

Limp Binding in which boards are not used. Paperbacks could technically be described as having a limp binding, but in practice the term is normally only used for books bound without boards in cloth or imitation cloth.

List A publisher's list of titles – "We are glad to announce that X has joined our list", or "Our list contains general non-fiction and medical books, but does not include fiction."

Literal The equivalent in composition of a typing error. In America the term "typo" is used.

Net Under the Net Book Agreement, books must not be sold to the public at less than the price fixed by the publisher, which is the "net" price. Most books published in Britain are "net", though school text books are frequently "non-net". Bookclubs can offer net books at a discount because of the conditions they attach to membership.

Ozalids   Proofs of highly illustrated books often come in the form of "Ozalids". Authors are often appalled by them, but should be reassured that they do not reflect the quality of the finished printing. Since Ozalids are usually blue, they are often referred to as "blues".

Paper   Three main kinds of paper are used for books: antique, a fairly rough-surfaced paper, used for most books without integrated tonal illustrations; calendered paper, which has been subjected to a smoothing process, used for illustrated books; art paper, coated with china clay or other material to give a glossy surface for the fine printing of illustrations.

Paper sizes   The most popular sizes of paper for books are Metric Crown, Metric Large Crown, Metric Demy and Metric Royal, of which quad sheets (i.e. sheets four times the basic sizes) measure in millimetres 768×1008, 816×1056, 888×1128 and 960×1272 respectively. The terms "quarto (4to)", "octavo (8vo)", "sixteenmo (16mo)" and so on refer to the number of times the basic sheet of paper is folded to produce a signature; quarto is folded twice, producing a Crown page size, for instance, of 252×192mm; octavo is folded three times, producing a Demy page size, for instance, of 222×141mm; and so on. Paper is used not only in quad sheets, but in larger sizes, and also in reels.

Paste-up   A paste-up is usually prepared for highly illustrated books, taking the proofs of the text and of the illustrations and pasting them into the blank pages of a dummy to show the printer the exact position required.

Perfect binding   See Binding.

Point size   The size of type is indicated in points, this showing the height of the block on which the individual letter stands. So one refers to "10pt type" or "36pt type". A point equals approximately $\frac{1}{72}$ inch.

Prelims   The first or preliminary pages of a book, including title-page, biblio-page, contents, etc, before the text begins.

Printing processes   There are three main printing methods in general use: letterpress, in which type or blocks, or metal or plastic plates are used, the ink being spread over them and the paper applied to the inked type – basically the same method that Caxton used; offset lithography and rotogravure both involve photography of printed pages or illustrations and the creation from the film of printing surfaces. Some books are printed "flatbed", the type remaining level and often stationary, and others are printed "rotary", the type having been made into curved plates which are fitted on to a cylinder which prints the paper as it rotates.

Print run　　The number of copies of a book printed at any one time.

Proofs　　Proofs come in various forms. Galley proofs are long strips of paper on which long columns of print, not yet split up into pages, appear. Paged galleys are also long strips of paper, but the columns of type on them have been split into pages, though these have not yet been imposed. Other proofs look like computer print-outs. Page proofs normally look much like paperbacks, the type having been split into pages and the pages imposed.

Recto　　Open a book: the left-hand page is called the "verso"; the right-hand page is called the "recto".

Remainder　　When a publisher finds that one of his books appears to have stopped selling, he may try to sell off his stock at a very low price to certain traders who specialize in such purchases. Books sold in this way are called "remainders" and the people who buy them are "remainder merchants". The word "remainder" is also a verb – "I shall have to remainder these books."

Running head　　The headline at the top of a page. Sometimes the title of a book is repeated on all pages, but more often the book title appears on the verso and the chapter title or title of a sub-section on the recto.

Sheets　　When a book is printed the sheets have to be folded and collated before the book can be bound. Sometimes, however, the publisher does not wish to bind all the copies that he has printed at that point in time, and he may keep part of his stock in the form of either flat or folded and collated sheets. Sheets may also be sold unbound – to library suppliers, for instance – and in many co-editions the originating publisher will supply the other publishers concerned with sheets rather than bound stock.

Signature　　When a printed sheet has been folded into pages it is called a "signature".

Spine　　The back of a book, and especially the back of the binding case, frequently rounded.

Subscription   When a publisher sells his books to booksellers and other trade outlets prior to publication he "subscribes" them. Such advance sales are "subscription" sales. The word "subscription" is also used to mean the total number of copies of a book sold before publication – "This book has had a good subscription."

Subsidiary rights   All rights in a book other than those of the original publisher to produce his own editions of the book.

Title   Apart from the obvious meaning of the name of a book, publishers use this word as a synonym for "book" – "I am publishing twenty titles this Spring."

Verso   See Recto.

Widow   A short line appearing as the first line of a new page. Typographers dislike "widows". Equally they dislike "club lines" – the first line of a paragraph appearing as the last line on a page.

Wrapper   See Jacket.

Index